AF559758

COMMUNITY TOURISM
AND
NATURAL RESOURCE CONSERVATION

COMMUNITY TOURISM AND NATURAL RESOURCE CONSERVATION

By

David Carr

DISCOVERY PUBLISHING HOUSE PVT. LTD.
NEW DELHI-110 002

Published by:

DISCOVERY PUBLISHING HOUSE PVT. LTD.
4383/4B, Ansari Road, Darya Ganj
New Delhi-110 002 (India)
Phone : +91-11-23279245; 23253475; 43596065
E-mail : discoverybooksindia@gmail.com
discoverypublishinghouse@gmail.com
namitwasan9@gmail.com
web : www.discoverypublishinggroup.com

***First Published:* 2011**
***Reprinted:* 2022**

ISBN: 978-81-8356-939-2

Community Tourism and Natural Resource Conservation

Printed at:
Infinity Imaging Systems
Delhi

PREFACE

The Community Based Tourism Institute (CBT-I) in Thailand works with hill tribe and coastal villagers who for years have had no say in how they are visited on trekking holidays to ensure that they have full management over these visits and homestays. They are working with 50 local communities and the visits on offer are very good examples of enjoyable and fascinating holidays where local people are really benefiting. Community Tourism is a new phenomenon. It is a spirit that permeates all sectors of the tourism industry. In other words it is a philosophy around which tourism products are developed.

It is about new levels of relationships between the host country and the visitor. What is appealing to the visitor is found among the varied natural attractions, local resources and talents, and indigenous attributes of a community or area. Through visitor-community interaction, respective cultures are explored, ideas and information are exchanged, and new friends are made. Community Tourism fosters opportunities at the community level for local people wishing to participate more fully in the tourism industry. This may range from establishing bed & breakfast accommodation in a rural home to creating income-generating tourism opportunities for an entire village.

Preserving natural resource and habitat is the utmost task for those countries which are encouraging tourists to visit their country. Community-based tourism is sharing the natural resources of a local community with local and foreign tourists for the sustainable devlopment of that local community whilst conserving the natural environment and respecting the way of life. This tourism is a growing market, as new generations of travellers worldwide seek more meaningful experiences from their leisure time. It is an opportunity for every country which boasts a wealth of natural beauty, cultural and spiritual heritage and fascinating multi-ethnic communities in addition to the traditional appeal of natural landscapes. This book will inspire and guide to readers and travelers alike who have firm faith in sustainable development.

—Author

CONTENTS

CHAPTER-1

INTRODUCTION

Community-based tourism is a growing market, as new generations of travellers worldwide seek more meaningful experiences from their leisure time. Sarvodaya believes it is an opportunity for Sri Lanka, a country which boasts a wealth of natural beauty, cultural and spiritual heritage and fascinating multi-ethnic communities in addition to the traditional appeal of her beaches.

Traditional beach and site-seeing tourism is vital to Sri Lanka's economy but, some argue, it does not always benefit and engage the communities which surround the hotels. The CTI is designed to empower, engage and financially sustain communities without in any way compromising their traditions, values and way of life. At the same time, each site and experience is conceived, developed and marketed to ensure its appeal and accessibility to the visitors and, in turn, its sustainability in benefiting the community.

Community tourism (sometimes called community-based tourism) is a form of tourism which aims to include and benefit local communities, particularly indigenous peoples and villagers in the rural South (ie 'developing world'). For instance, villagers might host tourists in their village, managing the scheme communally and sharing the profits. There are many types of community tourism project, including many in which the 'community' works with a commercial tour operator, but all community tourism projects should give local people a fair share of the benefits/profits and a say in deciding how incoming tourism is managed.

These tours open up a world of adventure and opportunity. Visit the Amazon...trek through the Andes or the Sinai... experience the magic of the central Australian desert... Good community-based tours take you beyond mainstream tourism. You'll meet people from different countries and learn far more about them and their culture than on conventional tours. You'll feel better knowing that your visit is genuinely helping your hosts. And if you want to simply lie on a beach.... well, there are tours here that feature some of the best beaches on the planet.

You'll find a more detailed discussion of community tourism in Tourism Concern's book, The Ethical Travel Guide, as well as more complete descriptions of the tours in the directory. Click here to buy the book!

Community tourism should...

- Be run with the involvement and consent of local communities.

  (Local people should participate in planning and managing the tour.)

- Give a fair share of profits back to the local community.

  (Ideally this will include community projects (health, schools, etc).)

- Involve communities rather than individuals.

  (Working with individuals can disrupt social structures.)

- Be environmentally sustainable

  (Local people must be involved if conservation projects are to succeed.)

- Respect traditional culture and social structures.
- Have mechanisms to help communities cope with the impact of western tourists.
- Keep groups small to minimise cultural / environmental impact.

- Brief tourists before the trip on appropriate behaviour.
- Not make local people perform inappropriate ceremonies, etc.
- Leave communities alone if they don't want tourism.

(People should have the right to say 'no' to tourism.)

The Community Based Tourism Institute (CBT-I) in Thailand works with hill tribe and coastal villagers who for years have had no say in how they are visited on trekking holidays to ensure that they have full management over these visits and homestays. They are working with 50 local communities and the visits on offer are very good examples of enjoyable and fascinating holidays where local people are really benefiting.

PRINCIPLES OF COMMUNITY TOURISM

Community Tourism is a new phenomenon. It is a spirit that permeates all sectors of the tourism industry. In other words it is a philosophy around which tourism products are developed.

Community Tourism is about new levels of relationships between the host country and the visitor. What is appealing to the visitor is found among the varied natural attractions, local resources and talents, and indigenous attributes of a community or area. Through visitor-community interaction, respective cultures are explored, ideas and information are exchanged, and new friends are made.

Community Tourism fosters opportunities at the community level for local people wishing to participate more fully in the tourism industry. This may range from establishing bed & breakfast accommodation in a rural home to creating income-generating tourism opportunities for an entire village.

Community Tourism is managed tourism in its profoundest sense, taking into account evolving travel trends in such areas as the environment, study and research, seniors travel and other special interests.

Community Tourism products and services are geared to address these trends and to satisfy the interests of emerging travel markets. Key clientele includes:

- The mature market
- Study and Research groups, including schools, universities, colleges and research based organizations
- Church groups
- Environmentalists, botanist, ornithologists and nature lovers
- The independent traveler
- Afro-Americans
- Caribbean Nationals - at home and abroad

The vision of Community Tourism is to expose the local resources and talents, and make the concept a reality for local people. Community Tourism embraces eco-tourism, cultural tourism, adventure tourism, recreational tourism, geo-tourism, heritage tourism, health tourism, farm tourism and all the popular special interest tourism.

Community-based Ecotourism

Thanks to funding from the United Nations Development Program and other NGO's, small rural communities are the owners of exciting new tourism projects. They are proud to share their beautiful waterfalls, their rainforest reserves, and their delicious country cuisine with visitors. In turn, ecotourism allows them to supplement their farming income while protecting their watersheds and providing meaningful employment near home. Now you can visit these great destinations with your own bilingual naturalist guide/driver.

Nacientes Palmichal-Palmichal is a small mountain town with hiking and horse back trails to the cloud forest reserve which protects the community's watershed. The town is untouched by tourism and is very much like the Costa Rica of years ago. The community is conservation-minded: several families use biodigestors to produce methane for cooking.

Reserva Los Campesinos-This welcoming agricultural community has several gorgeous waterfalls. You get close to the largest one on a 127-meter hanging bridge across a canyon. In two-hour guided hike, your hosts teach you about the riches of the rainforest as you climb to a mirador, with views of the Pacific coastline. Halfway up the trail, a pulley-car zips you across a gorge. When you get back from your hike, a pristine waterfall pool offers a refreshing dip. Spacious cabins have views across the canyon. Their rustic dining room serves delicious country cooking ($45 for meals, lodging and hikes). Reserva Los Campesinos is in Quebrada Arroyo, about an hour (25 km) inland from Quepos and Manuel Antonio. It's best to have 4WD to drive there yourself, or you can hire a 4WD taxi to take you there for about $50 round trip per taxiload.

El Copal Reserve and Lodge- The 190-hectare El Copal Reserve, between Orosi and Turrialba, has beautiful primary forest, home to almost 400 species of birds. In nearby El Humo de Pejivalle there are several trapiches, where visitors can observe the fascinating process by which the local hard brown sugar is made.

Other attractions in the area are Guayabo National Monument, Costa Rica's largest preColumbian archaeological site; Irazu and Turrialba volcanoes; Tapanti National Park; the famous orchid collection at Lankester Gardens; the charming Orosi church; Cartago's Basilica, home to Costa Rica's patron saint, La Virgen de los Angeles; whitewater rafting and kayaking.

Tesoro Verde-The women of Los Planes, a small community four kilometers uphill from Drake Bay, turned a former Park Headquarters into a charming inn with room for 15 guests. They will take you hiking in Corcovado National Park, in their own rainforest reserve, to nearby waterfalls or snorkeling at Isla del Cano.

Uganda Community Tourism Association

UCOTA exists to help poor communities improve their lives through the sale of handicrafts and the provision of accommodation, guiding and cultural performances. Every time you buy a UCOTA craft or service, you are helping UCOTA member to help themselves! At the same time, you receive a unique product or service in return!

UCOTA has 33 member groups countrywide involved in handcrafts production and selling. Women constitute 99% of these groups and are located in rural impoverished communities that depend on subsistence agriculture and have very low income generating opportunities.

The handcrafts produced by these UCOTA members of different types depending on culture and locally available raw materials. The handcraft types include pottery, paper mache,' beads, tie and dye, wood curving, hand-made paper, basketry, bark cloth, etc.

All the handcraft products made by the UCOTA members are organic. The raw materials used are farm residues and some are forest products. UCOTA assists the handcraft producers to grow the forest raw materials on their farms to avoid the possible depletion of these materials from the natural resources.

The income from the handcrafts supplements family revenue and it is used to meet essential family needs like clothing, food, school dues and scholastic materials for children, health costs etc.

In some instances, a small percentage of the selling price is deducted from each craft sold, and is a contribution to the community development fund which is used to implement community development projects like schools, health clinics, immunization, mobile clinics, adult literacy classes etc.

Community-based Tourism Development

Community-based development is a strategy used by tourism planners to mobilize communities into action to participate in broadening the scope of offerings in the industry. The goal is socio-economic empowerment and a value-added experience for local and foreign visitors.This process opens new niches for destination Jamaica, most notably for the nature, culture, and adventure traveler.

The concept existed in Jamaica for many years at an informal level, where visitors sought a 'home away from home' with Jamaican families - participating in, and learning about the Jamaican way of life while experiencing warm Jamaican hospitality.This fostered greater interactivity, built cross cultural bonds, respect and understanding, and gave authenticity to Jamaican lifestyles, while creating a source of income for the host families.

Tourism-based development has now been formalized as a developmental tool for building not only the tourism industry, but the entire country, by opening up communities as attractions with definable modus operanda with achievable goals. The process is guided by industry standards of health, safety and regard for the environment.What this achieves is a policy objective of creating a culture of inclusion in the industry, whereby communities participate and share in the wealth of the industry, dispelling a long held perception of tourism as an exploiter of wealth where only the rich can benefit.

Community-based development empowers people to be more aware of the value of their community assets - their culture, heritage, cuisine and lifestyle. It mobilizes them to convert these into income generating projects while offering a more diverse and worthwhile experience to visitors. Every citizen is a potential business partner to be trained in small business management, environmental awareness, product development and marketing.This type of 'people-centred' tourism promotes a sense of 'ownership' which augurs well for the industry's sustainability.

The Tourism Product Development Company has been actively involved in formulating, implementing and acting as a catalyst for community-based development and offers this guide for project development and implementation.

Community Tourism on Jamaica's Southwest Coast

In Jamaica, a country where tourism is a major industry, foreign travelers bring much needed income to a depressed national economy. However, the spread of this revenue has become a sore spot for many local small business owners. Annually, many tourist dollars are soaked up by all-inclusive resorts at commercial epicenters such as Montego Bay, Ochos Rios, and Negril. While these resorts do hire some local employees, many fear that money from tourists flows right back into the hands of foreign investors rather than into the local economies. Communities also suffer because of the likelihood of guests choosing to stay within the limits of their hotel due to fear of crime and violence on the island. In response to these perceived threats to Jamaica's prosperity, many groups are trying to organize local tourism projects to draw visitors away from larger resort locations.

Travel to some of these smaller outlying areas can provide an exciting and inexpensive alternative to an average vacation package as well as a more realistic sense of Jamaican culture.

For tourists traveling in Jamaica's southwestern-most parish of Westmoreland, the popular destination in recent years has become Negril, a laid-back resort town 52 miles west of Montego Bay. A small fishing village only twenty years ago, it is now a Mecca for Spring Break debauchery among American twenty-somethings.

Pristine beaches that once ran, uninterrupted, into the cliffs on the west point of the island have now been broken up by buoyed markers that outline the backyards of a plethora of all-inclusive resorts.

One interested in taking a walk on the sands is now more likely to trip over sunburned tourists and be waylaid by drug dealers than enjoy a peaceful jaunt.

Worst of all, visitors to this completely Americanized concrete jungle are much more inclined to meet hustlers and prostitutes, there only to prey on tourists, than the 3,000 hardworking locals who tend to remain hidden from view. This is the main cause behind many misconceptions about Jamaican people and tends to perpetuate negative stereotypes about their society.

For those island travelers looking for peace and quiet, as well as a more realistic glimpse of a rich and varied culture, a trip eastward on highway A2, along the south coast of the parish, can be a wonderfully educational experience.

The first step toward really experiencing Jamaica is to get away from the tourist spots. There are many ways of traveling throughout the island, but I would recommend using the taxis and minibuses found at hubs referred to as "bus stops", though they are not for everyone. These are the transport of choice for most locals and are much less expensive than chartered taxis, although many are unregistered and one should always keep track of their belongings. In Negril, the best way of reaching one of these "bus stops" is to flag down another taxi in town and have them drop you off. It will probably cost you more for the ride through Negril than it will to travel across the entire parish, however. Once at the aforementioned location, you won't have any trouble finding a ride.

While you're wading through a sea of white Toyota Corolla hatchbacks, various drivers yell their destinations and try to entice you into riding with them.

Beware the chartered taxi drivers on the street who will try to charge you exorbitant prices for their service. When in doubt, look to see whom the locals are jumping in with.

Your initial destination will be Savanna-La-Mar or 'Sav', a medium sized town of 16,000 and the capital of Westmoreland, located roughly a half-hours drive away, depending on the lunacy of your particular driver. While the chartered taxi drivers would try to trick you into paying $60 US, you shouldn't have to pay more than $1 US for the fare.

If anyone tries to get you to pay more, haggle and tell them that you "know what go on!" This will usually win you the local fare, but expect the local accommodation as well. Fitting four people in the back seat is not unusual!

A ride in a taxi on Jamaican roads can be a frightening experience. The highways themselves are actually very narrow, with intermittent one-lane bridges and a constant influx of goats, cattle, and dogs crossing from one side to the other. The roads are also the main thoroughfares for pedestrians who walk and ride bicycles on both sides without the luxury of a sidewalk. To make matters worse, Jamaican drivers, especially the taxi drivers, usually push the top speed on their vehicles in an attempt to make better time, and it is not unusual to find oneself hurtling around a hairpin turn on a one-lane road at over 100 km/hr. This is why Jamaica has one of the highest highway fatality rates in the world. However, while many of the drivers are reckless, their skill is undeniable, and your only available recourse is usually to just roll down the window, forget the danger, and enjoy the ride. One consolation is that the roads out of Negril are some of the best on the island, especially the short ride east through the plains of Westmoreland.

In no time, you'll find yourself exiting the vehicle at another depot in Savanna-La-Mar, windblown and shaking from the wild ride, and immediately being shuffled toward another taxi. Don't forget to pay the first driver when you get out. Always pay when the ride is over, and make sure you have all your belongings out of the vehicle before you do so. If you want to continue your journey toward the coast, young men standing on the street will help you find the correct taxi, but if you are so inclined, Savanna-La-Mar can be a fun place to explore as well. You'll have to find another driver to take you into the downtown area, but you'll have no trouble finding one of those either, and it won't cost you nearly as much as the ride through Negril.

Savannah-La-Mar, a concrete jungle in its own right, is nonetheless a polar opposite from Negril. The city itself is built around Great George Street, a wide thoroughfare, just over a mile long, that hails from the days of British presence on the island. It has been the site of several hurricanes over the years, yet still boasts a wide variety of historical sites including a fountain that was once at the center of the town, the original courthouse, and several historic churches. This road leads to a rustic downtown district lined with shops and filled with the hustle and bustle of everyday traffic. Unlike in the tourist areas of Montego Bay, Ochos Rios and Negril, these shops are not filled with vacationers, and one would actually be hard up to find a pink face or flowered shirt in the entire area. The drug dealers and hustlers of Negril are nowhere to be found, 'Rastas' and school children being the most represented demographic. Though you might think that this would cause you to stand out as the only tourist, it is really more likely that you will be ignored than approached on the streets.

Overall, Savannah-La-Mar is a great place to do some shopping for local goods and observe the fast pace of a Jamaican city during an average day. As the biggest community in the area, it is also a good spot to exchange currency at a bank or "cambio", stop by a grocery store or pharmacy, or pick up any other needed supplies. It would also be a good idea to save your souvenir shopping until you've reached Sav and the other communities further down the road. You're much more likely to purchase an authentic piece of art in outlying areas than in the tourist towns. It's not unusual for people to buy a piece of artwork in Negril that is supposed to be an original and see the same piece further down the beach or notice the 'Made in Taiwan' sticker too late. While this is an obvious benefit of escaping crowds, Sav isn't a tourist area for good reason, and those seeking fun and sun would be better served to move on down the coast, possibly returning periodically for the amenities provided by the urban setting.

The local nightlife is not ideal for travelers either. There is a disco called Club Safari in town that is pretty lively on Thursday nights (which are ladies nights across most of the island), and though it isn't comparable to the Negril nightclubs, it is much more of a local scene. If you go, keep your wits about you and your money in a safe place. There is also a go-go club on the eastern outskirts of town called Club Cancer, which ironically has an ad for a local brand of cigarettes hanging over the sign. Travelers beware... these clubs are a mixture between strip clubs and brothels and attract a very bad crowd. Such locations can be dangerous places and it would be unwise to attend without a local escort.

After a few hours on the hot pavement in town, you'll probably be ready to head further down A2 toward the beach communities. A cab or a brisk walk will take you to your point of origin. Another taxi or minibus will gladly whisk you into the eastside of the parish, but remember to plan on arriving before dark. Most taxis finish in late afternoon, and after that you're looking at an expensive chartered ride because other forms of transport (e.g. hitchhiking) can be very dangerous after the sun is down. Once again, the ride shouldn't cost more than $1 US and it can be a very enjoyable trip, depending on the number of people riding with you and the ability of the driver.

After Savanna-La-Mar, your route will take a southward turn along the thin eastern coast of Westmoreland. It is a beautiful drive. As all traces of the urban setting are left behind, rolling green mountains, thick with foliage, end in sheer limestone cliffs, which drop off into the thick mangrove swamps bordering the coast. The climate is drier than other parts of the island and a forgiving breeze often floats off the sea. Soon, the beach will become visible as the road wraps around Bluefields Bay. The communities surrounding this area are the outermost of the parish and some of the most comfortable on the island. There is no better area to experience the sleepy seaside culture of the southern coast.

If you would like to stay in the Bluefields Bay area, accommodations should be your first order of business. Although it's always best to make reservations in advance, rooms are not all that difficult to come by, and there shouldn't be much of a problem unless it's December through March and the peak of tourist season. Hoteliers in the area provide a wide range of options for where to stay, and prices truly run the spectrum. In the village of Bluefields, as well as in neighboring Belmont, your choices are basically either budget or top-end accommodations. Sunset Cottages (876-955-8007) is located on the ocean side of A2 and provides simple rooms with a view for only $20-50 US per night. Just across the street at Belmont Garden Cottages (876-955-8138), one can have the pleasure of staying in the 'yard' of elderly Mr. Forrester, whose roomy cottages and kindness always make for a pleasant stay at $25 apeice. A little further down the road, at the Belmont Cabins, one can also find a decent room, at under $25 US and have the added amenity of Gooden's tropical restaurant and bar. As for more luxurious lodging options, there are several villas in the area run by Braxton and Debbie Moncure (202-232-4010) which provide full service and privacy, but at the expense of thousands of dollars per week.

As far as food and entertainment are concerned, the scene in Bluefields is definitely low key. For barbecue, the jerk stands at the Bluefields Beach Park are a good place for lunch. Pablo's Paradise is also a great place to eat and provides a nice drinking atmosphere in the evenings for tourists. Further down the road, KD's Keg and Fish Joint provides decent food and a nice beachside locale in which to have a cocktail and play a couple games of pool. Gooden's, just across the street, is also a popular local hangout with a limited daily menu. When ordering Jamaican food, there will probably be a lot of fish and chicken served, along with 'rice and peas' (what we would call 'red beans and rice') and starchy vegetables. Some of the food is spicy and may take time to get used to, but for the most part it is very healthy and cheap at around $5 US per meal. For a smaller snack, baked pastries called 'patties' are found at many locations and cost less than $1 US apiece. Those found at the pastry shop in Belmont are exceptional.

Most locals prepare their own food, so restaurants aren't all that common, but neighborhood shops, located every 100 ft. or so, offer a wide variety of produce and supplies. Beer and rum is often served, as well, and such stores can become sites of lively dominoes play after dark. Having a good time at these establishments, or at any of the bars along the road, is usually very safe at night though one should be wary of drivers because the roadway is poorly lit.As anywhere, women should take extra precautions, possibly traveling in pairs. Sometimes, Jamaican men can come on very strong, leading to uncomfortable situations. For the most part, however, locals are easy-going and quick to make friends with you, but don't be surprised when you're asked to buy a few drinks. Also, it's not unusual if every place seems empty in the evening as many Jamaicans don't go out until midnight and parties can last until dawn.

Unless there is some sort of local event or special occasion, however, the nightlife in the area really isn't anything to write home about. The main attractions in the community are the beautiful beaches along the coastline. Though some are located on private property, there are several public beaches that are just as nice. The Bluefields Beach Park is one, but it can get a bit crowded on Sundays, and there are many other options. The best way to find your favorite spot is to do some old fashioned exploring. Some beaches will have more rocks than others, and some will be marshier, or have more trash. One method of finding a good swimming hole is to go where the fishermen dock their boats. They usually tie up on sandy beaches, and you might get to see someone bring in the day's catch. Boat traffic is usually very slow, but it is always a good idea to be careful.

If you are interested in fishing, many locals will be happy to take you out with them, but it will usually cost you around $40 US an hour for their time and gas. If you go, remember to find a guide who you can understand well so that you can ask questions. It's also wise to go through someone recommended by whoever you are staying with. They may cost a bit more, but you'll know they're reliable and others will know where you're going. Also, make sure you specify what type of fishing you would like to try. Techniques vary from pulling traps and using nets along the beach to line fishing several miles out. Also, lifejackets are rare and the sea is unpredictable, so make sure you are up to the task. Taking a little Dramamine for motion sickness before leaving is always smart. Sunscreen and water are also imperative.

For those in search of an extreme experience, tuna fishing can be particularly exhilarating. Boats usually head out to sea before dawn, and by sunrise, a brave soul could find themselves several miles out as Jamaica disappears beyond the horizon. Once all traces of land have faded away, you'll be busy simply trying to stay in the boat and keep your breakfast down as the tiny vessel pitches and rolls in the bright blue water. While cruising through the waves, the fishermen let out lines tied to nothing more than plastic bottles and wait to hit a school of fish. The anticipation often becomes unbearable, but rest assured, 10 lbs. spiny creatures will soon be flying onto the floor of the boat and flapping like mad until you realize that it's your job to knock them senseless and deposit them into the cooler. If you happen to go out on a good day, you can look forward to fresh grilled tuna back on the beach.

Other excursions include less formal tours into the foothills of the local agricultural communities. "Ganja" or marijuana is the major cash crop in the eastern half of Westmoreland and many farmers use it to supplement their normal subsistence crops. Some individuals, many of them Rastafarians, choose to grow ganja full time. Most of these fields are hidden far in the hills and are worked by a co-op of local men. It is possible to find a guide to these distant sites, but you should be very cautious. The cultivation of ganja is illegal in Jamaica, and police harassment is common. Also, Rastas are very suspicious of foreigners, especially men who are curious about their business. You'll have to earn the trust of the person you go with, and the adventure will cost you in either money or labor. You may also have to hike through some rough terrain to reach the hidden location. Make sure you know what you're getting yourself into before tromping off into the 'bush' with a stranger and his machete.

A guided tour of historical sites in the area can also be very interesting and somewhat less dangerous. The Bluefields Bay area of Westmoreland has a rich past, having been a haven for Spanish and British boats and even pirate vessels including those of the infamous Henry Morgan. Later, English and Scottish colonists occupied many of the bay's environs, cultivating indigo and later sugar cane in large quantities. Sugar production later became the paramount industry on the island,

and a plantation system developed under which great numbers of slaves were inhumanely imported from Africa. While the demand for cane sugar later ebbed, a lasting impression has remained in the land, and its people. Sugar cane is still grown in the area in small quantities, and several local plantation houses are still standing. A trip to any of these locations usually provides a lovely ride, as well as a greater sense of understanding and compassion for Jamaicans.

Currently, the political climate in Bluefields Bay and its surrounding communities is rather serene. Since the US supported ganja eradication of 1986, and aside from occasional drug busts and isolated acts of violence, recent history in the region has been somewhat uneventful. Belmont and Bluefields are actually somewhat conservative and haven't yet developed the more commercial lifestyles prevalent in the popular metropolitan areas. Due to the old-fashioned and laid-back attitude typical of the of locals, time spent there can be profoundly relaxing and days seem to fly by as one slowly falls in step with the pace of small-town life. The attitude can be summed up in the connotation of a favorite phrase of many Jamaicans who promise to "soon come" and then don't return soon at all. Remember, if you're impatient you'll drive yourself crazy, but once you can learn to relax, you'll have the time of your life.

Unfortunately, the local lifestyle may be endangered as looming plans for the future development of all-inclusive resorts in the district threaten entrepreneurs and homeowners in close proximity. In response to possible changes in the commercial sector, many of the 7,000 residents of the local Bluefields Bay communities have been pulling together to organize community tourism projects to help small-business owners and bring more money into the community. This type of community development is the main emphasis of the Bluefields People's Community Association (876-955-8792) formed in the late 1980's by Terry Williams, and continued today by Keith Wederburn and Wolde Kristos (876-421-7449).

With the help of these and other local resources, you should be able to plan a fun and relaxing vacation, and though you surely won't want to leave, you'll be confident that you've had a unique experience when you do. When finally ready to vacate the area, several options exist. You could always trace your steps and head back west to Negril, though after your experience on other parts of the island, that might not seem so appealing. Further to the east lie the Black River, YS Falls, Treasure Beach, and even Kingston. Minibuses and taxis are available on the southeast part of the island, but the journey would be a grueling one and a chartered ride much more comfortable. To the north lies the Cockpit Country of Trelawney and the road to Montego Bay, both journeys where a chartered taxi would probably be necessary though, as always, it will be cheaper than in Negril.

Whether going home or on to some new adventure, as you speed away from Jamaica's beautiful southwest coast, leaving Bluefields Bay and its surrounding communities behind, you're sure to reflect on the time you've stayed. In all likelihood, your stay will have been comfortable. You'll have had the opportunity to try exotic new foods and probably will have consumed too much local rum on more than one occasion. You'll smile as you look back on the various adventures you've had fishing, visiting historical sites, or wandering through fields of ganja. Also, after spending everyday on the beach and eating only fish and produce, you'll look and feel wonderful. Moreover, you'll have made many new friends and can say that you've experienced real Jamaican culture. Best of all, you can do all of this while still having some money in your pocket when the trip is over, confident that what you did spend while in Jamaica went right where it belongs, to the Jamaicans.

Tourism Planning Resources

The following inventory of tourism development resources is organized with the community development practitioner in the Lake States in mind. The websites listed in Comprehensive Resources provide such a wealth of links and tourism resources that they should be listed first. We have duplicated many of their links, but have chosen a different annotation and organization scheme. Tools are resources - usually manuals, guidebooks, tool kits, or web-based system - that provide practical advice, guidance, or analysis. Information Resources provide links to publications and web content that allow the user to develop a better understanding of different components of the tourism industry.

Tourism Industry Organizations

American Hotel & Lodging Association	Organization representing hotel and lodging establishments with a primary focus on advocacy in Washington, D.C.
American Resort Development Association	Organization dedicated to serving and promoting the resort and timeshare industry in the U.S. Includes publications for sale.
Hospitality Sales and Marketing Association International	Member-based organization with resources and services to serve the hospitality industry worldwide.
International Association of Convention and Visitor Bureaus	Organization serving the destination management professional. Includes links to other industry organizations and publications for sale.
Travel and Tourism Research Association	Organization serving travel research and marketing professionals. Includes a bi-monthly e-journal on travel research.
Travel Business Roundtable	Organization which considers itself the leading voice on government tourism policy in Washington. Includes publicati-

	ons on national tourism policy and economic impacts.
Travel Industry Association of America	Organization dedicated to promoting and research the entire travel industry. Also based in Washington, D.C.
World Tourism Organization	Specialized agency of the UN dedicated to promoting tourism worldwide and a leader in measuring and researching international tourism statistics.
World Travel and Research Council	Organization representing private tourism business interests worldwide.

CHAPTER-2

IDENTITY, COMMUNITY AND SUSTAINABILITY

IDENTITY

Put at its simplest, identity is a very personal concept for each of us. It defines who or what we think we are. Easily said, but often we feel like we don't know who we or what we're doing. This isn't strange, although it is a little worrying. Much of the reason we feel like we're unsure of our identity lies with the rapidly changing nature of society around us. The things that used to help us define who we are -- church, family, community, nation, school, and so on -- have been undermined or debased. This is a prime reason behind the crisis of identity felt by many of us.

Of course, not all of these aspects of identity were necessarily good. Strong feelings of association with a particular country, political belief, or racial group can lead to very negative feelings about members of other groups. This can lead to racism, excessive nationalism, xenophobia, and so on. All the same, human beings seem to need some sort of strong identification with a particular group or collective culture. So if the old collective identities are being broken down, new ones must be forming in different places, and one of these places may well be in cyberspace.

At the level of the individual, identity and trust are prerequisites for collaboration and community betterment. And the Net facilitates group communication more readily than inter-group, diminishing its utility to address local needs.

Psychologists use "identity" to describe personal identity, or the idiosyncratic things that make a person unique. Sociologists use "social identity" to describe group membership. In community governance "identity" is used in this later sense while incorporating the trust that comes with eye-to-eye familiarity with an individual. On the internet, identity and trust are more difficult to discern. (Our Security and Privacy page examines these problems.) Efforts like OpenID are working to bridge the internet's identity and trust gap. But first, let's take a look at identity from a more tradition public policy perspective. (The following borrows heavily from Identity Politics by Rick Muir.)

From a public policy perspective, identity is tied in with social cohesion. There are three main approaches to improving social cohesion, all of which play a distinctive role.

- First is legislation. The most critical element here is the anti-discrimination and equalities legislation that outlaws discrimination on grounds of religion, race, sexuality, gender, disability and age. Achieving legal equity and driving out discrimination and prejudice are fundamental prerequisites for social cohesion.
- Second is economic and social policy. Socio economic inequalities in New York City are stark and exist along ethnic, racial, and class lines. A society cannot be at ease with itself with such inequalities. Social disadvantage also creates an environment in which low-income families are forced to compete for scarce resources, such as jobs, childcare, and affordable housing. Material scarcity and perceptions of unfairness in how such scarce goods are distributed play an important role in generating an atmosphere of hostility towards asylum seekers and migrants more generally. The hard social democratic graft of tackling disadvantage and promoting equal life chances is therefore a fundamental precondition of cohesion.
- The third approach to tackling identity and social cohesion relates to cultural change. People's relations

with one another are affected by the beliefs and practices through which they understand themselves and organize their lives. There are three main approaches to develop cohesion through cultural change: shared action, shared values, and shared identity.

The credibility of the messenger is critical if people are to buy into a shared identity. As things stand, politicians are probably the least trusted messengers we have. Under these circumstances, how do we build identity?

- First, interaction between citizens is in itself a basic building block for an inclusive civic identity. As contact theory has shown, in order for people to identify with citizens from a different background to their own, meaningful contact across cultural boundaries is important.
- Second, given the importance of symbols and narratives in identity formation, we need to reassess the way we represents identity. If we are to construct a genuinely inclusive and shared identity, symbols need to reflect the multicultural nature of our society. This means, for example, addressing the role of community boards and local civic organizations. The kind of public monuments we put up, the figures we commemorate and events we celebrate should also reflect the culturally diverse heritage of our great city.
- Third, we need to find new sources of collective identity that all New Yorkers can share. Recent focus group work by ippr found that there is a tendency among white participants to reach for exclusive sources of national identity when asked what they would like to celebrate. If we are to avoid exclusive conceptions, we need to find sources of identity that all New Yorkers will find appealing. Here are a few possibilities.

- First is New York's democratic and humanitarian heritage. Almost everyone in our society values democracy. It is one of the things that provides an effective way of marrying our two desirable goals of diversity and cohesion. Because it provides the space in which our various different identities can flourish, democracy is intimately connected with the celebration of cultural diversity. In appealing to democracy as a basis for shared identity, we would be fostering pride in the framework that makes cultural pluralism possible. And by integrating the tools of the Internet with traditional democratic traditions we will connect the atomic and subatomic.
- A second progressive source of identity would be diversity and multi-culturalism. For example, in New York's Olympic bid, our cultural, ethnic and racial diversity was a major source of pride and clearly central to the bid. We might present our identification with humanity as a whole, rather than with the nation. A popularly held global cosmopolitan identity seems a natural course of progression in the UN headquarters city.
- A third source of shared identity is culture in the narrower sense of the word: music, media, the visual arts, and drama. Culture is our business. And artists themselves are putting on new forms of public art specifically aimed at engaging large audiences, such as, in 2005, the Gates Project in Central Park.
- Finally, there is our built heritage. New York City's landmark areas, its skyscrapers, parks, and entertainment venues are world class.

Shared identity has the potential to make a valuable contribution to social cohesion through its ability to foster affective ties between potentially quite large numbers of people. It can thus help us to meet people's desire for a shared sense of belonging, something that other approaches to cohesion lack.

People will find their own way of relating to their communities, the city, and nation and some will resist identifying with these spheres altogether - this is inevitable. But if we wishe to foster cohesion in the public interest, we can provide the framework that makes shared identification among residents possible. Rather than approaching identity in a top-down fashion that would almost inevitably backfire, we should see its role as setting the structural framework that makes it more likely that shared identities will develop.

While the government should ensure that the way our schools operate, our communities function and housing developments are planned encourage people to mix with others from different backgrounds to their own, we shoulkd strive to create an online environment that facilitates parallel developments. We should create interaction-based initiatives to break down barriers between the groups. We should ensure that our symbols, rituals and the civic calendar reflects our cultural diversity and include culturally diverse narratives that make up community history. We should seek out new sources of identity around which residents of all backgrounds can share some common ground.

Security

Only a global engagement can insure security on a global network. We have engaged in providing for the security of New Yorkers on the Internet through our participation in ICANN and the Kantara Initiative. "In the real world, we use social constructs to create an environment that is "safe enough," one sufficiently secure and predictable that we are prepared to live in it. It is through participation in a collective social sphere that we achieve this sense of safety. Zittrain points out that to make the Internet a "safe enough" place, we need to put into practice theories of security that allow us to depend on our friends, share insights and observations with others, and establish a socially embedded online experience. This shift is a key part of rethinking security and should be the target of serious consideration. "

Trust

Trust is the oil that makes both social and commercial relationships run more smoothly. Our focus here is on the oils that benefit community and civic relationships. (For information on the .nyc TLD's role in facilitating commercial trust.

Without trusted relationships, civil society comes undone. A key map to the importance and role of trust to civil society was presented in the Augmented Social Network (ASN) paper written in 2003 by Ken Jordan, Jan Hauser, and Steven Foster. In ASN, they wrote:

While the ASN paper had an emphasis on global online world, our focus is on a limited geographic entity. Our trust must bridge the digital and atomic worlds of real people and traditional processes.

Community

Inventing new technology is not essential to improve community and civic communication. For example, a simple cooperative directory of civic groups and calendar of activities will facilitate their operation. One goal of .nyc is to provide short, descriptive, memorable names for local community and civic organizations and to facilitate their use. Perhaps, with its tight geographical space, as we develop networking tools, we'll discover that we live in a small city with four or three degrees of separation.

Justice

The Free Dictionary provides the following definitions for justice:

- The quality of being just; fairness.
- The principle of moral rightness; equity.
- Conformity to moral rightness in action or attitude; righteousness.

- The upholding of what is just, especially fair treatment and due reward in accordance with honor, standards, or law.
- Law The administration and procedure of law.
- Conformity to truth, fact, or sound reason: The overcharged customer was angry, and with justice.

When we have identity, trust, community, and justice, we have all the reasons in the world to have -

Civic Pride

According to the Free Dictionary, pride, has good and bad sides. Here are the main definitions:

- A sense of one's own proper dignity or value; self-respect.
- Pleasure or satisfaction taken in an achievement, possession, or association: parental pride.
- Arrogant or disdainful conduct or treatment; haughtiness.

The broad goal of .nyc is to enable residents to have pleasure and satisfaction in civic achievement without haughtiness. As we better communicate, as we create a just society, we can begin to feel civic pride.

Civic Networks

We envision social networks providing key building blocks for the city's future well being. With adequate networks we may no longer be a city ruled by calamity: Reporter - "What's our next priority?" Official, "Let me find out what's collapsed and I'll get back to you." The Voter Project offers an opportunity for developing a civic network.

Other Benefits

- Educated and aware community.
- Technical training.
- Privacy & Security

Concerns

- Privacy - A key concern is privacy. Cities were traditionally a place where people could get lost in the crowd. But privacy is difficult to protect as cameras and blogs and cell phones and search and mining and photosynth and GIS merge. Take a look at the history and scope of the issue of global privacy as interpreted by Peter Fleischer: Leadership comes from Europe and its experiences in WW 2. With the U.S. understandably anxious aaro the 9/11 disaster; there's little leadership from the government. But any solution must be global in nature.
- It was reported in the Boston Globe that in Robert Putnam's latest work (not yet formally released in the U.S.) indicates that mixed-immigrant communities exhibit a lesser degree of civic cooperation than more homogeneous communities. Perhaps game theory might shed some light on how best to approach a situation of this sort. Exercises in no-zero sum situations might be worthwhile explorations.

Concepts of Collective Identity:

So how do we see ourselves and each other? Here are some ideas:

- People band themselves together imaginatively in groups; you may as a person have a number of identities (national, gender, local/city, race) and different aspects of your collective identity are important to you than others.
- Identity is therefore not fixed or given; this fights against dominant Western notion of the fixed, autonomous self.
- Identity is constantly reconsituted and in constant flux; you are being reconstituted as are the collectives you define yourself against.

SOCIAL IDENTITY (THEORY)

One approach toward identity that is grounded in psychology has gained academic currency in recent years. Known broadly as social identity theory, the focus here is on the centrality of social identity as a factor in individuals' sense of self-identity.

This social identity is essentially a categorization framework made up of sets of comparisons and contrasts used to emphasize distinctions among groups. It suggests an active process whereby collectives proactively form "in-groups" by setting themselves apart from others; in so doing, the group cements relationships among members of the in-group while providing individuals with a sense of belonging within the collective (Tajfel & Turner, 1986; Hogg & Abrams, 1988).

A crucial aspect of this theory is the fluctuating nature of identity. While people tend to identify with many social groups, based on various factors such as race, ethnicity, class, gender, national origin, and so on, these factors become salient at different times and in different ways. According to social identity theory, if and when a particular group identity becomes salient at a particular time - for whatever reason - the sentiments, emotions, and behaviors of any given member of the salient group will tend to be affected and guided by the norms and aspirations of that group.

Crisis of Identity

Because the things that used to help us define who we are -- family, community, etc. -- have been undermined in recent decades, people talk about a crisis of identity we are all supposed to be suffering from. This is primarily a poststructuralist concept, since its effects seem to have been arisen with the changes in society brought about by poststructuralism and postmodernism. Here's how:

- From 1960s onwards dominant structuralism began to be replaced by micropolitics, lobby groups, localism, nationalism, etc., interms of group identity.

The breakdown of the old order led to crises of identity and representation, and a loss of old identities at the collective level. So Jameson, for example, argues that the subject in a postmodern world is not alienated, but rather fragmented.

- "Alientation presumes a central, unitary self . . . [b]ut if, as a postmodernist sees it, the self is decentered and multiple, the concept of alienation breaks down. All that is left is the anxiety of identity" (Turkle, 1995: 49).

So How Did This Happen?

- Two things were happening at the same time in the 1960s:
  - (a) This was the beginning of the end of the modernist dominant theory thesis and traditional ideas about hegemony. Micropolitics arrives.
  - (b) Lacan begins writing about the decentered self, attacking the notion of an embedded self.
- By beginning of the 1970s, the question "Who am I?" becomes harder to answer at both an individual and collective level. By the 1970s-80s, you see the beginnings of new collectives being formed (Yuppies, DINKies, etc.)

  Now, instead of experiencing, achieving or learning we're more likely to buy and consume our identity. Consumer culture was around earlier but now it has intensified, almost taken over. How do you get an authentic identity? Is it possible at all or is identity being undercut by the postmodern phenomenon?

Postmodernity and Identity:

- Modernity changed the sense of identity through urban revolution.
- In postmodernity, although the city experience is still important, the mass media are more important in changing sense of individual and cultural identity.

- People who are positive about postmodernism point to crushing of individual identity in modern city design to show how postmodernity supposedly brings back importance (this argument works best in architecture).
- Globalization started as an economic phenomenon and ends as a phenomenom of identity. (E.g., Scottish nationalists might be lumped in with the problems in Bosnia and the Basque country).

Identity and New Media

As Sherry Turkle puts it: "Many of the institutions that used to bring us together -- a main street, a union hall, a town meeting -- no longer work as before. Most people spend most of their day alone at a screen of a television or a computer. Meanwhile, social beings that we are, we are trying (as Marshall McLuhan said) to retribalize. And the computer [and new media] is playing a central role."

Performance, Identity and Community

The relationships between performance, identity and community are of significant critical concern in theatre and performance studies. This working group explores the ways performance can allow constituencies of interest to be realised and to gain social efficacy.

The group understands that each of our three key terms is complex, and that the terms and consequences of their intersection pose challenges for both critical and political practice. We wish to encourage research that engages the rubric of the group inventively and interrogatively, building on a number of key issues and problems:

- The basis on which performance may be linked with concerns of identity and community
- The ways in which relationships between performance, identity and community are materialised and gain theatrical and social efficacy

- The intersection between performance, civil society and democracy
- The historical and geographical inscription of this relationship
- The challenges and opportunities for critical practice posed by examining this relationship.

Sustainability

Sustainability is the capacity to endure. In ecology, the word describes how biological systems remain diverse and productive over time. Long-lived and healthy wetlands and forests are examples of sustainable biological systems. For humans, sustainability is the potential for long-term maintenance of well being, which has environmental, economic, and social dimensions.

Healthy ecosystems and environments provide vital goods and services to humans and other organisms. There are two major ways of reducing negative human impact and enhancing ecosystem services. The first is environmental management; this approach is based largely on information gained from earth science, environmental science, and conservation biology. The second approach is management of human consumption of resources, which is based largely on information gained from economics.

Sustainability interfaces with economics through the social and ecological consequences of economic activity. Sustainability economics involves ecological economics where social, cultural, health-related and monetary/financial aspects are integrated. Moving towards sustainability is also a social challenge that entails international and national law, urban planning and transport, local and individual lifestyles and ethical consumerism. Ways of living more sustainably can take many forms from reorganising living conditions (e.g., ecovillages, eco-municipalities and sustainable cities), reappraising economic sectors (permaculture, green building, sustainable agriculture), or work practices (sustainable architecture), using science to develop new technologies (green technologies, renewable energy), to adjustments in individual lifestyles that conserve natural resources.

The word sustainability is derived from the Latin sustinere (tenere, to hold; sus, up). Dictionaries provide more than ten meanings for sustain, the main ones being to "maintain", "support", or "endure". However, since the 1980s sustainability has been used more in the sense of human sustainability on planet Earth and this has resulted in the most widely quoted definition of sustainability and sustainable development, that of the Brundtland Commission of the United Nations on March 20, 1987: "sustainable development is development that meets the needs of the present without compromising the ability of future generations to meet their own needs."

At the 2005 World Summit it was noted that this requires the reconciliation of environmental, social and economic demands - the "three pillars" of sustainability. This view has been expressed as an illustration using three overlapping ellipses indicating that the three pillars of sustainability are not mutually exclusive and can be mutually reinforcing.

The UN definition is not universally accepted and has undergone various interpretations. What sustainability is, what its goals should be, and how these goals are to be achieved are all open to interpretation. For many environmentalists the idea of sustainable development is an oxymoron as development seems to entail environmental degradation. Ecological economist Herman Daly has asked, "what use is a sawmill without a forest?" From this perspective, the economy is a subsystem of human society, which is itself a subsystem of the biosphere, and a gain in one sector is a loss from another. This can be illustrated as three concentric circles.

A universally accepted definition of sustainability is elusive because it is expected to achieve many things. On the one hand it needs to be factual and scientific, a clear statement of a specific "destination". The simple definition "sustainability is improving the quality of human life while living within the carrying capacity of supporting eco-systems", though vague, conveys the idea of sustainability having quantifiable limits. But sustainability is also a call to action, a task in progress or "journey" and therefore a political process, so some definitions set out common goals and values. The Earth Charter speaks of "a sustainable global society founded on respect for nature, universal human rights, economic justice, and a culture of peace."

To add complication the word sustainability is applied not only to human sustainability on Earth, but to many situations and contexts over many scales of space and time, from small local ones to the global balance of production and consumption. It can also refer to a future intention: "sustainable agriculture" is not necessarily a current situation but a goal for the future, a prediction. For all these reasons sustainability is perceived, at one extreme, as nothing more than a feel-good buzzword with little meaning or substance but, at the other, as an important but unfocused concept like "liberty" or "justice". It has also been described as a "dialogue of values that defies consensual definition".

Environmental Dimension-Healthy ecosystems provide vital goods and services to humans and other organisms. There are two major ways of reducing negative human impact and enhancing ecosystem services and the first of these is environmental management. This direct approach is based largely on information gained from earth science, environmental science and conservation biology. However, this is management at the end of a long series of indirect causal factors that are initiated by human consumption, so a second approach is through demand management of human resource use.

Management of human consumption of resources is an indirect approach based largely on information gained from economics. Herman Daly has suggested three broad criteria for ecological sustainability: renewable resources should provide a sustainable yield (the rate of harvest should not exceed the rate of regeneration); for non-renewable resources there should be equivalent development of renewable substitutes; waste generation should not exceed the assimilative capacity of the environment.

At the global scale and in the broadest sense environmental management involves the oceans, freshwater systems, land and atmosphere, but following the sustainability principle of scale it can be equally applied to any ecosystem from a tropical rainforest to a home garden. In March 2009 at a meeting of the Copenhagen Climate Council, 2,500 climate experts from 80 countries issued a keynote statement that there is now "no excuse" for failing to act on global warming and that without strong carbon reduction targets "abrupt or irreversible" shifts in climate may occur that "will be very difficult for contemporary societies to cope with". Management of the global atmosphere now involves assessment of all aspects of the carbon cycle to identify opportunities to address human-induced climate change and this has become a major focus of scientific research because of the potential catastrophic effects on biodiversity and human communities.

Other human impacts on the atmosphere include the air pollution in cities, the pollutants including toxic chemicals like nitrogen oxides, sulphur oxides, volatile organic compounds and particulate matter that produce photochemical smog and acid rain, and the chlorofluorocarbons that degrade the ozone layer. Anthropogenic particulates such as sulphate aerosols in the atmosphere reduce the direct irradiance and reflectance (albedo) of the Earth's surface. Known as global dimming, the decrease is estimated to have been about 4% between 1960 and 1990 although the trend has subsequently reversed. Global dimming may have disturbed the global water cycle by reducing evaporation and rainfall in some areas. It also creates a cooling effect and this may have partially masked the effect of greenhouse gases on global warming.

Water covers 71% of the Earth's surface. Of this, 97.5% is the salty water of the oceans and only 2.5% freshwater, most of which is locked up in the Antarctic ice sheet. The remaining freshwater is found in glaciers, lakes, rivers, wetlands, the soil, aquifers and atmosphere. Due to the water cycle, fresh water supply is continually replenished by precipitation, however there is still a limited amount necessitating management of this resource. Awareness of the global importance of preserving water for ecosystem services has only recently emerged as, during the 20th century, more than half the world's wetlands have been lost along with their valuable environmental services. Increasing urbanization pollutes clean water supplies and much of the world still does not have access to clean, safe water. Greater emphasis is now being placed on the improved management of blue (harvestable) and green (soil water available for plant use) water, and this applies at all scales of water management.

Ocean circulation patterns have a strong influence on climate and weather and, in turn, the food supply of both humans and other organisms. Scientists have warned of the possibility, under the influence of climate change, of a sudden alteration in circulation patterns of ocean currents that could drastically alter the climate in some regions of the globe. Ten per cent of the world's population - about 600 million people - live in low-lying areas vulnerable to sea level rise.

Loss of biodiversity stems largely from the habitat loss and fragmentation produced by the human appropriation of land for development, forestry and agriculture as natural capital is progressively converted to man-made capital. Land use change is fundamental to the operations of the biosphere because alterations in the relative proportions of land dedicated to urbanisation, agriculture, forest, woodland, grassland and pasture have a marked effect on the global water, carbon and nitrogen biogeochemical cycles and this can impact negatively on both natural and human systems. At the local human scale, major sustainability benefits accrue from sustainable parks and gardens and green cities.

Since the Neolithic Revolution about 47% of the world's forests have been lost to human use. Present-day forests occupy about a quarter of the world's ice-free land with about half of these occurring in the tropics. In temperate and boreal regions forest area is gradually increasing (with the exception of Siberia), but deforestation in the tropics is of major concern.

Food is essential to life and feeding more than six billion human bodies takes a heavy toll on the Earth's resources. This begins with the appropriation of about 38% of the Earth's land surface and about 20% of its net primary productivity. Added to this are the resource-hungry activities of industrial agribusiness - everything from the crop need for irrigation water, synthetic fertilizers and pesticides to the resource costs of food packaging, transport (now a major part of global trade) and retail. Environmental problems associated with industrial agriculture and agribusiness are now being addressed through such movements as sustainable agriculture, organic farming and more sustainable business practices.

The underlying driver of direct human impacts on the environment is human consumption. This impact is reduced by not only consuming less but by also making the full cycle of production, use and disposal more sustainable. Consumption of goods and services can be analysed and managed at all scales through the chain of consumption, starting with the effects of individual lifestyle choices and spending patterns, through to the resource demands of specific goods and services, the impacts of economic sectors, through national economies to the global economy. Analysis of consumption patterns relates resource use to the environmental, social and economic impacts at the scale or context under investigation. The ideas of embodied resource use (the total resources needed to produce a product or service), resource intensity, and resource productivity are important tools for understanding the impacts of consumption. Key resource categories relating to human needs are food, energy, materials and water.

The Sun's energy, stored by plants (primary producers) during photosynthesis, passes through the food chain to other organisms to ultimately power all living processes. Since the industrial revolution the concentrated energy of the Sun stored in fossilized plants as fossil fuels has been a major driver of technology which, in turn, has been the source of both economic and political power. In 2007 climate scientists of the IPCC concluded that there was at least a 90% probability that atmospheric increase in CO2 was human-induced, mostly as a result of fossil fuel emissions but, to a lesser extent from changes in land use. Stabilizing the world's climate will require high-income countries to reduce their emissions by 60-90% over 2006 levels by 2050 which should hold CO2 levels at 450-650 ppm from current levels of about 380 ppm. Above this level, temperatures could rise by more than 2°C to produce "catastrophic" climate change. Reduction of current CO2 levels must be achieved against a background of global population increase and developing countries aspiring to energy-intensive high consumption Western lifestyles.

Reducing greenhouse emissions, referred to as decarbonization, is being tackled at all scales, ranging from tracking the passage of carbon through the carbon cycle to the commercialization of renewable energy, developing less carbon-hungry technology and transport systems and attempts by individuals to lead carbon neutral lifestyles by monitoring the fossil fuel use embodied in all the goods and services they use.

Water security and food security are inextricably linked. In the decade 1951-60 human water withdrawals were four times greater than the previous decade. This rapid increase resulted from scientific and technological developments impacting through the economy - especially the increase in irrigated land, growth in industrial and power sectors, and intensive dam construction on all continents. This altered the water cycle of rivers and lakes, affected their water quality and had a significant impact on the global water cycle. Currently towards 35% of human water use is unsustainable, drawing on diminishing aquifers and reducing the flows of major rivers: this percentage is likely to increase if climate change impacts become more severe, populations increase, aquifers become progressively depleted and supplies become polluted and unsanitary. From 1961 to 2001 water demand doubled - agricultural use increased by 75%, industrial use by more than

200%, and domestic use more than 400%. In the 1990s it was estimated that humans were using 40-50% of the globally available freshwater in the approximate proportion of 70% for agriculture, 22% for industry, and 8% for domestic purposes with total use progressively increasing.

Water efficiency is being improved on a global scale by increased demand management, improved infrastructure, improved water productivity of agriculture, minimising the water intensity (embodied water) of goods and services, addressing shortages in the non-industrialised world, concentrating food production in areas of high productivity, and planning for climate change. At the local level, people are becoming more self-sufficient by harvesting rainwater and reducing use of mains water.

The American Public Health Association (APHA) defines a "sustainable food system" as "one that provides healthy food to meet current food needs while maintaining healthy ecosystems that can also provide food for generations to come with minimal negative impact to the environment. A sustainable food system also encourages local production and distribution infrastructures and makes nutritious food available, accessible, and affordable to all. Further, it is humane and just, protecting farmers and other workers, consumers, and communities." Concerns about the environmental impacts of agribusiness and the stark contrast between the obesity problems of the Western world and the poverty and food insecurity of the developing world have generated a strong movement towards healthy, sustainable eating as a major component of overall ethical consumerism. The environmental effects of different dietary patterns depend on many factors, including the proportion of animal and plant foods consumed and the method of food production. The World Health Organization has published a Global Strategy on Diet, Physical Activity and Health report which was endorsed by the May 2004 World Health Assembly. It recommends the Mediterranean diet which is associated with health and longevity and is low in meat, rich in fruits and vegetables, low in added sugar and limited salt, and low in saturated fatty acids; the traditional source of fat in the Mediterranean is olive oil, rich in monounsaturated fat. The healthy rice-based Japanese diet is also high in carbohydrates and low in fat. Both diets are low in meat and saturated fats and high in legumes and other vegetables; they are associated with a low incidence of ailments and low environmental impact.

At the global level the environmental impact of agribusiness is being addressed through sustainable agriculture and organic farming. At the local level there are various movements working towards local food production, more productive use of urban wastelands and domestic gardens including permaculture, urban horticulture, local food, slow food, sustainable gardening, and organic gardening.

As global population and affluence has increased, so has the use of various materials increased in volume, diversity and distance transported. Included here are raw materials, minerals, synthetic chemicals (including hazardous substances), manufactured products, food, living organisms and waste.

Sustainable use of materials has targeted the idea of dematerialization, converting the linear path of materials (extraction, use, disposal in landfill) to a circular material flow that reuses materials as much as possible, much like the cycling and reuse of waste in nature. This approach is supported by product stewardship and the increasing use of material flow analysis at all levels, especially individual countries and the global economy.

Synthetic chemical production has escalated following the stimulus it received during the second World War. Chemical production includes everything from herbicides, pesticides and fertilizers to domestic chemicals and hazardous substances. Apart from the build-up of greenhouse gas emissions in the atmosphere, chemicals of particular concern include: heavy metals, nuclear waste, chlorofluorocarbons, persistent organic pollutants and all harmful chemicals capable of bioaccumulation. Although most synthetic chemicals are harmless there needs to be rigorous testing of new chemicals, in all countries, for adverse environmental and health effects. International legislation has been established to deal with the global distribution and management of dangerous goods.

Every economic activity produces material that can be classified as waste. To reduce waste industry, business and government are now mimicking nature by turning the waste produced by industrial metabolism into resource. Dematerialization is being encouraged through the ideas of industrial ecology, ecodesign and ecolabelling. In addition to the well-established "reduce, reuse and recycle" shoppers are using their purchasing power for ethical consumerism.

Social dimension-Sustainability issues are generally expressed in scientific and environmental terms, but implementing change is a social challenge that entails, among other things, international and national law, urban planning and transport, local and individual lifestyles and ethical consumerism."The relationship between human rights and human development, corporate power and environmental justice, global poverty and citizen action, suggest that responsible global citizenship is an inescapable element of what may at first glance seem to be simply matters of personal consumer and moral choice."

Social disruptions like war, crime and corruption divert resources from areas of greatest human need, damage the capacity of societies to plan for the future, and generally threaten human well-being and the environment. Broad-based strategies for more sustainable social systems include: improved education and the political empowerment of women, especially in developing countries; greater regard for social justice, notably equity between rich and poor both within and between countries; and intergenerational equity. Depletion of natural resources including fresh water increases the likelihood of "resource wars". This aspect of sustainability has been referred to as environmental security and creates a clear need for global environmental agreements to manage resources such as aquifers and rivers which span political boundaries, and to protect global systems including oceans and the atmosphere.

According to Murray Bookchin, the idea that humans must dominate nature is common in hierarchical societies. Bookchin contends that capitalism and market relationships, if unchecked, have the capacity to reduce the planet to a mere resource to be exploited. Nature is thus treated as a commodity: "The plundering of the human spirit by the market place is paralleled by the plundering of the earth by capital." Still more basically, Bookchin argued that most of the activities that consume energy and destroy the environment are senseless because they contribute little to quality of life and well being. The function of work is to legitimize, even create, hierarchy. For this reason understanding the transformation of organic into hierarchical societies is crucial to finding a way forward.

Social ecology, founded by Bookchin, is based on the conviction that nearly all of humanity's present ecological problems originate in, indeed are mere symptoms of, dysfunctional social arrangements. Whereas most authors proceed as if our ecological problems can be fixed by implementing recommendations which stem from physical, biological, economic etc., studies, Bookchin's claim is that these problems can only be resolved by understanding the underlying social processes and intervening in those processes by applying the concepts and methods of the social sciences.

Deep ecology establishes principles for the well-being of all life on Earth and the richness and diversity of life forms. This is only compatible with a substantial decrease of the human population and the end of human interference with the nonhuman world. To achieve this, deep ecologists advocate policies for basic economic, technological, and ideological structures that will improve the quality of life rather than the standard of living. Those who subscribe to these principles are obliged to make the necessary change happen.

One approach to sustainable living, exemplified by small-scale urban transition towns and rural ecovillages, seeks to create self-reliant communities based on principles of simple living, which maximise self-sufficiency particularly in food production. These principles, on a broader scale, underpin the concept of a bioregional economy. Other approaches, loosely based around new urbanism, are successfully reducing environmental impacts by altering the built environment to create and preserve sustainable cities which support sustainable transport. Residents in compact urban neighbourhoods drive fewer miles, and have significantly lower environmental impacts across a range of measures, compared with those living in sprawling suburbs.

Ultimately, the degree of human progress towards sustainability will depend on large scale social movements which influence both community choices and the built environment. Eco-municipalities may be one such movement. Eco-municipalities take a systems approach, based on sustainability principles. The eco-municipality movement is participatory, involving community members in a bottom-up approach. In Sweden, more than 70 cities and towns-25 per cent of all municipalities in the country-have adopted a common set of "Sustainability Principles" and implemented these systematically throughout their municipal operations. There are now twelve eco-municipalities in the United States and the American Planning Association has adopted sustainability objectives based on the same principles.

There is a wealth of advice available to individuals wishing to reduce their personal impact on the environment through small, inexpensive and easily achievable steps. But the transition required to reduce global human consumption to within sustainable limits involves much larger changes, at all levels and contexts of society. The United Nations has recognised the central role of education, and have declared a decade of education for sustainable development, 2005-2014, which aims to "challenge us all to adopt new behaviours and practices to secure our future". The Worldwide Fund for Nature proposes a strategy for sustainability that goes beyond education to tackle underlying individualistic and materialistic societal values head-on and strengthen people's connections with the natural world.

CHAPTER-3

ENVIRONMENTAL STANDARDS

The quality of the environment, both natural and man-made, is essential to tourism. However, tourism's relationship with the environment is complex. It involves many activities that can have adverse environmental effects. Many of these impacts are linked with the construction of general infrastructure such as roads and airports, and of tourism facilities, including resorts, hotels, restaurants, shops, golf courses and marinas. The negative impacts of tourism development can gradually destroy the environmental resources on which it depends.

On the other hand, tourism has the potential to create beneficial effects on the environment by contributing to environmental protection and conservation. It is a way to raise awareness of environmental values and it can serve as a tool to finance protection of natural areas and increase their economic importance.

HOW TOURISM CAN CONTRIBUTE TO ENVIRONMENT

The tourism industry can contribute to conservation through:

Financial Contributions

- **Direct financial contributions**—Tourism can contribute directly to the conservation of sensitive areas and habitat. Revenue from park-entrance fees and similar sources can be allocated specifically to pay for the protection and management of environmentally sensitive areas. Special fees for park operations or conservation activities can be collected from tourists or tour operators.

- **Contributions to government revenues**—Some governments collect money in more far-reaching and indirect ways that are not linked to specific parks or conservation areas. User fees, income taxes, taxes on sales or rental of recreation equipment, and license fees for activities such as hunting and fishing can provide governments with the funds needed to manage natural resources. Such funds can be used for overall conservation programs and activities, such as park ranger salaries and park maintenance.

For Costa Rica, for example, tourism represents 72% of national monetary reserves, generates 140,000 jobs and produces 8.4% of the gross domestic product. The country has 25% of its territory classified under some category of conservation management. In 1999, protected areas welcomed 866,083 national and foreign tourists, who generated about US$ 2.5 million in admission fees and payment of services.

Improved Environmental Management and Planning

Sound environmental management of tourism facilities and especially hotels can increase the benefits to natural areas. But this requires careful planning for controlled development, based on analysis of the environmental resources of the area. Planning helps to make choices between conflicting uses, or to find ways to make them compatible. By planning early for tourism development, damaging and expensive mistakes can be prevented, avoiding the gradual deterioration of environmental assets significant to tourism.

Cleaner production techniques can be important tools for planning and operating tourism facilities in a way that minimizes their environmental impacts. For example, green building (using energy-efficient and non-polluting construction materials, sewage systems and energy sources) is an increasingly important way for the tourism industry to decrease its impact on the environment. And because waste treatment and disposal are often major, long-term environmental problems in the tourism industry, pollution prevention and waste minimization techniques are especially important for the tourism industry. A guide to sources of information on cleaner production (free) is available here.

Environmental Awareness Raising

Tourism has the potential to increase public appreciation of the environment and to spread awareness of environmental problems when it brings people into closer contact with nature and the environment. This confrontation may heighten awareness of the value of nature and lead to environmentally conscious behavior and activities to preserve the environment. For instance, Honduran schoolchildren from the capital city of Tegucigalpa are routinely taken to visit La Tigra cloud forest visitor center, funded in part by eco-tourist dollars, to learn about the intricacies of the rainforest.

If it is to be sustainable in the long run, tourism must incorporate the principles and practices of sustainable consumption. Sustainable consumption includes building consumer demand for products that have been made using cleaner production techniques, and for services - including tourism services - that are provided in a way that minimizes environmental impacts. The tourism industry can play a key role in providing environmental information and raising awareness among tourists of the environmental consequences of their actions. Tourists and tourism-related businesses consume an enormous quantity of goods and services; moving them toward using those that are produced and provided in an environmentally sustainable way, from cradle to grave, could have an enormous positive impact on the planet's environment.

Protection and Preservation

Tourism can significantly contribute to environmental protection, conservation and restoration of biological diversity and sustainable use of natural resources. Because of their attractiveness, pristine sites and natural areas are identified as valuable and the need to keep the attraction alive can lead to creation of national parks and wildlife parks.

In Hawaii, new laws and regulations have been enacted to preserve the Hawaiian rainforest and to protect native species. The coral reefs around the islands and the marine life that depend on them for survival are also protected. Hawaii now has become an international center for research on ecological systems - and the promotion and preservation of the islands' tourism industry was the main motivation for these actions.

Grupo Punta Cana, a resort in the Dominican Republic, offers an example of how luxury tourism development and conservation can be combined. The high-end resort was established with the goal of catering to luxury-class tourists while respecting the natural habitat of Punta Cana. The developers have set aside 10,000 hectares (24,700 acres) of land as a nature reserve and native fruit tree garden. The Punta Cana Nature Reserve includes 11 fresh water springs surrounded by a subtropical forest where many species of unusual Caribbean flora and fauna live in their natural state. Guests can explore a "nature path" leading from the beach through mangroves, lagoons of fresh water springs and dozens of species of Caribbean bird and plant life. The Punta Cana Ecological Foundation has begun reforesting some parts of the reserve that had been stripped of their native mahogany and other trees in the past. Other environmentally protective policies have been put into effect at the resort, such as programs to protect the offshore barrier reefs and the recycling of wastewater for use in irrigating the grounds. The fairways of the resort's new golf course were planted with a hybrid grass that can be irrigated with sea water The grass also requires less than half the usual amounts of fertilizer and pesticides. The resort has also established a biodiversity laboratory run by Cornell University.

Tourism has had a positive effect on wildlife preservation and protection efforts, notably in Africa but also in South America, Asia, Australia, and the South Pacific. Numerous animal and plant species have already become extinct or may become extinct soon. Many countries have therefore established wildlife reserves and enacted strict laws protecting the animals that draw nature-loving tourists. As a result of these measures, several endangered species have begun to thrive again.

Alternative Employment

Tourism can provide an alternative to development scenarios that may have greater environmental impacts. The Eco-escuela de Español, a Spanish language school created in 1996 as part of a Conservation International project in the Guatemalan village of San Andres, is an example. The community-owned school, located in the Maya Biosphere Reserve, combines individual language courses with home stay opportunities and community-led eco-tours. It receives around 1,800 tourists yearly, mostly from the US and Europe, and employs almost 100 residents, of whom around 60% were previously engaged in mostly illegal timber extraction, hunting and milpas, or slash-and-burn agriculture. Careful monitoring in 2000 has shown that, among the families benefiting from the business, the majority has significantly reduced hunting practices, and the number and extension of "slash-and-burn" agricultural plots. Furthermore, as most families in the village benefit directly or indirectly from the school, community-managed private reserves have been established, and social pressure against hunting has increased.

Regulatory Measures

Regulatory measures help offset negative impacts; for instance, controls on the number of tourist activities and movement of visitors within protected areas can limit impacts on the ecosystem and help maintain the integrity and vitality of the site. Such limits can also reduce the negative impacts on resources. Limits should be established after an in-depth analysis of the maximum sustainable visitor capacity. This strategy is being used in the Galapagos Islands, where the number of ships allowed to cruise this remote archipelago is limited, and only designated islands can be visited, ensuring visitors have little impact on the sensitive environment and animal habitats.

Effects of Other Industries on Tourism

Impacts from other industries often have a more dramatic effect on the environment and can seriously affect tourism.

- Oil spills, like the oil tanker disaster that occurred off the Galapagos Islands (Ecuador) in January 2001, can cause severe short-term damage to tourist attractions. In that case, a freight ship loaded with 160,000 gallons of diesel fuel and 80,000 gallons of other petroleum products ran aground on the coast of San Cristóbal and spilled nearly all of its load. Unique local marine and land species and the tourism potential of the area were badly affected.
- Agricultural runoff or industrial discharges can cause water pollution and may cause algae blooms like those that occurred in the Adriatic Sea in the early 1990s. In spite of improved control of sewage from tourism developments, the Mediterranean sea floor is increasingly carpeted with these quick-growing invaders, many rising 30 inches or more above anchoring runners. They appear equally adept at colonizing rock, mud, and sand in a virtually continuous swath that can extend from the beach out to a depth of about 150 feet, smothering coral reefs, fish and other sea flora and fauna in the process.
- Destructive practices such as blast fishing, fishing with poisonous chemicals like cyanide, and muro-ami netting (pounding reefs with weighted bags to scare fish out of crevices) directly destroy corals. They can also destroy a major draw for tourists.

Environmental Standards and Infrastructure Increasingly Determine Competitiveness In the Travel and Tourism Sector

Environmental protection, along with a modern transport infrastructure, are the factors which are increasingly determining the competitiveness of international destinations in the market for travel and tourism. Countries which include tourism more strongly in sustainable overall concepts can strengthen their position. That is one of the findings of the Global Travel & Tourism Competitiveness Report 2008 (TTCR). This second edition of the annual report has been prepared by the World Economic Forum in conjunction with the international strategy and technology consultants Booz & Company and other well-known partners. The report lists the 130 countries studied on an index assessing their competitiveness in the travel and tourism sector.

Recommendations from the last report were well-received by decision-makers in the tourism and tourist travel sectors; this is partly reflected in the form of practical changes whose effects can also be noted in the new ranking. Switzerland, Austria and Germany continue to top the list, particularly on account of their environmental standards (exemplary in international terms) and similarly exemplary transport infrastructure. Sweden has achieved a significant leap of nine places up the rankings, partly due to its heightened efforts on environmental issues. These same concerns also account for the good index rankings achieved by the other Scandinavian countries. Improvements are also noted for Brazil (up 10 places) and for two Mediterranean states, Spain (up 10 places) and Italy (up 5 places). Progress has also been achieved by other popular Southern European holiday destinations, such as Portugal (up 7 places) and Greece (up 5 places).

The Travel and Tourism Sector as the Driver of Regulatory Changes

A further finding of this report is that the travel and tourism sector is a key wealth driver for emerging countries like China and South Africa. These nations have used supportive legislation to decisively improve their competitiveness in these areas. China, which this year is staging the Olympic Games, achieved dramatic improvements in the ranking,, due to a combination or regulatory adjustments and infrastructure measures (up to 62nd in the ranking from 71 last year). South Africa also succeeded in moving up the rankings (to 60th spot, up from 62 last year); the country is set to be the first on the African continent to stage the Football World Cup, in 2010.

Countries with a Long-term Environmental Agenda Prominently Ranked

Countries placing a stronger emphasis on sustainability come out particularly well in the rankings, and Bulgaria is a good example of this. The country has developed concepts offering alternatives to package holiday tourism on the Black Sea coast. "Implementing strategies is one of the most important success factors in establishing a balance between short-term economic successes and long-term ecological objectives," says Jürgen Ringbeck, a managing partner with Booz & Company. He adds that customers will increasingly demand "green" tourism services. "The travel and tourism companies are now faced with the challenge of satisfying this demand."

EU States Amongst the Most Competitive when it Comes to Tourism

As a consequence of their advanced infrastructure, secure statutory framework conditions and high level of education and training, the industrialised nations again come out best in the ranking. Amongst the Top 10 of the total number of 130 countries studied for the TTCR, there is strong representation from Europe, which accounts for seven of the places. In addition to Switzerland (1), Austria (2) and Germany (3), the leading group includes Spain (5), Great Britain (6), Sweden (8) and France (10). Italy improved on its poor ranking of the previous year, rising to 28th spot in this year's index. However, in the European comparison this popular holiday destination continues to lag behind due to the high price level, relatively low safety standards and, above all, the poorly-developed mind-set in terms of protecting the environment.

The Study - approach Adopted and Presentation

In total, 130 countries around the world were studied, looking at over 60 variables. These included taking account of statutory regulations, health and safety, infrastructure, the local price level and cultural aspects. To acknowledge the growing influence of the environmental protection factor in tourism and tourist travel, the index was expanded to include specific analysis of the points "ecology and sustainability".

The full report can be downloaded at the World Economic Forum's homepage:

The results of the TCCR are being presented in detail at the ITB in Berlin. On 7 March 2008, a panel discussion is being held in Hall 7.1a between 15:00 and 16:00. Using comparative country analyses, the event and presentation will illustrate those factors which increase a country's competitiveness and the business decisions which ought to be derived from that evidence. Following the event, the speakers will be available to conduct more in-depth discussions.

Tourism and Community Development

Tourism plays an increasingly important role in the development of communities throughout the U.S. Lake States. The benefits of tourism include both tangible (e.g. job creation, state and local tax revenue, etc.) and less tangible (e.g. social structure, quality-of-life, etc.) community effects. In addition, tourism can, and often does, result in less desirable effects on the economic, social, and environmental fabrics of communities. These benefits and costs provide ample opportunity for creative public policy debate.

The University of Wisconsin - Extension (UWEX) has a long and rich history of developing and supporting partnerships throughout the state and the region. Significant tourism educational programs began more than 40 years ago with the work of Professor Isadore Fine and the UW - Madison School of Commerce. Fifteen years later, this initial programming effort was formalized through the formation of the Recreational

Resources Center (later named the Tourism Research & Resource Center). This center provided educational programming to assist in community-based tourism planning and applied research. The center was eliminated in 1996 after its budget was reallocated to the Wisconsin Department of Tourism.

Since 1996, many county-based Community, Natural Resource and Economic Development (CNRED) educators have continued to develop and deliver quality tourism programming throughout Wisconsin and beyond. In addition, there continues to be a modest support network of specialists that conduct applied research programs addressing tourism development. Examples of issues addressed in this programming include business development, marketing, outdoor recreation planning, natural resources and amenity-base development, heritage tourism, nature-based tourism, festivals and events, tourism economics, tourism infrastructure, traveler research, and hospitality training. These local, regional, and state-level tourism efforts can greatly benefit from sanction, guidance, support, and packaging in creating an overarching umbrella for CNRED Tourism Programs.

Tourism has been and will continue to be an important component of our social, economic, and environmental heritage. We endeavor to sharing expertise and practices that are transferable to communities in the Lake States and beyond. By doing so, we have an opportunity to establish collaborative networks to help strengthen community-based tourism education and applied research. The literature and web-based resources captured here provide an organizing component intent on fostering this engagement.

This clearinghouse of community tourism resources is created as an evolving resource. We are interested in your suggestions for additions and future directions. Please direct comments to us using the following contact information. We hope you find this useful.

Community Attitudes Towards Tourism Development

In light of empirical evidence indicating the many and varied impacts of tourism to host destinations, various authors (e.g. Andriotis and Vaughan 2003; Lankford and Howard, 1994, p.122) recommended a focus on residents' perceptions of the conditions and changes that may exist in host communities. As has been suggested by some authors (for example, Allen et al., 1988; Andriotis and Vaughan 2003; Lankford & Howard, 1994; Ritchie, 1988) a balance of residents' perceptions of the costs and benefits of tourism is considered a major factor in visitor satisfaction and is, therefore, vital for the success of the tourism industry. Thus, Allen et al. (1988, p. 16) propose that residents perceptions of, and attitudes towards tourism must be continually assessed to ensure that action is taken in good time and through such action the residents are willing partners in the development process. Going forward, awareness of residents' perceptions of tourism development and its impacts can help planners and developers to identify real concerns and issues in order for appropriate policies and action to take place, optimising the benefits and minimising the problems (Andriotis and Vaughan 2003).

Following the significance of community attitudes to the success of a destination, research on community attitudes toward tourists and tourism development has become one of the most systematic and well studied areas in the field of tourism. For instance, Andriotis and Vaughan (2003) have found 83 quantitative published papers in academic journals related to this area of research. Among these community attitudinal studies two frameworks have dominated:

- social exchange theory, that is concerned with "understanding the exchange of resources between individual and groups in an interaction of situation" where "actors supply one another with valued resources" (Ap 1992, p. 668), and
- social representations theory, that is concerned "with describing and understanding how and what people think in their ongoing everyday experiences and how a wider social reality influences these thoughts (Pearce, Moscardo, and Ross, 1996, p. 39)".

On the other hand, the majority of community studies have followed a quantitative approach. Within the extensive quantitative research on community attitudes, the majority applies statistical techniques without actually providing theory. Quantitative methods adopted in attitudinal research can be distinguished according to the statistical techniques they use as follows:

- bivariate or single factor approaches that investigate the influence of single factors, such as extrinsic (e.g. degree or stage of the host destination's development, type of tourists and seasonality), and intrinsic (e.g. distance that residents live from tourist zones, economic and/or employment dependency in tourism, length of residency, socio-demographic characteristics),
- multivariate or multiple factor approaches, (e.g. factor analysis and cluster analysis), which, unlike the bivariate, they examine more than one variable simultaneously and
- the ones that utilise both bivariate and multivariate methods.

Quality Tourism Standards

The Adventure Tourism Council began developing Quality Tourism Standards (QTS) in the early 1990's. Operators' main concerns were based around the need to raise and improve standards in the adventure tourism sector. Several draft codes of practice for various sectors have been developed over the years but until 1999 there had been no consensus on the development of a cost effective, practical solution that resolved administration, branding and marketing issues.

Global Situation-Internationally, quality-based standards are developing across all industry sectors, including tourism. These are typically centred around the international standards organisation series - including the ISO9000 (production) and ISO14000 (environmental) standards. Issues of liability, particularly the right to sue for compensatory and exemplary damages, and the potential effect of the European Travel Directive (European Union clients can sue New Zealand suppliers in their country of origin) are also driving the standards' development.

What are the Quality Tourism Standards?-The aim of QTS is to provide a client-focussed, cost effective, quality standard for providers of tourism products.

Seven different components within the QTS have been identified to date. These are:

- compliance
- safety
- environment
- cultural
- service
- training
- business
- facilities.

These are divided into sector-specific and generic components. Sector-specific components (e.g. safety) will be developed by the sectors themselves while generic components (e.g. environmental), will be facilitated by sector groups, TIANZ and other stakeholders.

So Who's Involved?-Below is a sample of the sector specific activities involved.

- Rafting
- Jetboating
- Horse-trekking
- Sea kayaking
- All-terrain vehicles
- Trekking
- Off-road vehicles
- Eco/nature tourism

- Adventure cycling
- Flight seeing
- Hunting

All of the above have generic components added to their own sector-specific components.

How Do They Work?-Qualmark will administer and market the QTS programme, and arrange for an annual independent accreditation of the operation. Accreditation will be based on the operator's implementation of the standard and result in the achievment of the Qualmark Visitor Activity Endorsement License. Successfully accredited companies will be able to market themselves as meeting the standard. They'll also be marketed domestically and internationally by Qualmark and, over time, visitor information centres will give these companies preferential treatment. It's also likely that Tourism New Zealand will make the QTS a minimum qualification for access to their website, international media programme and off-shore marketing.

CHAPTER-4

RESPONSIBLE TOURISM

Responsible tourism is an approach to the management of tourism, aimed at maximising economic, social and environmental benefits and minimising costs to destinations. Simply put, Responsible tourism is tourism 'that creates better places for people to live in, and better places to visit'. A responsible tourism approach aims to achieve the triple-bottom line outcomes of sustainable development, i.e. economic growth, environmental integrity and social justice. The distinguishing characteristic of the approach is the focus on the responsibility of role-players in the tourism sector, and destinations in general, to take action to achieve sustainable tourism development.

How Does the City of Cape Town Support Responsible Tourism?

The City of Cape Town has supported the principles of responsible tourism since the Cape Town Declaration in 2002. In 2004 it included them as a founding principle of Cape Town's Tourism Development Framework. In 2009 the City adopted the Responsible Tourism (RT) Policy and Action Plan. This plan will ensure that Cape Town is well on its way towards being a truly responsible destination. The City will exercise its mandate for local tourism through its sector leadership, facilitating and co-coordinating role, and the creation of a supportive policy environment and actions based on the economic, environmental and socio-economic principles of responsible tourism.

Tourism can take many forms across the world, but everyone involved in this industry (business, destinations and visitors) has a responsibility to ensure that tourism is a force for good. A force that sustains jobs, conserves cultural and natural heritage and provides fabulous experiences.

The Responsible Tourism Partnership

The Responsible Tourism Partnership works to help businesses and communities around the world to maximise their potential for responsible tourism through a range of activities and initiatives. The responsible tourism partnership work with

- tourism businesses in destinations & originating markets
- local & national governments
- local communities
- travel writers & journalists

The International Centre for Responsible Tourism

The ICRT is a postgraduate teaching and research centre at Leeds Metropolitan University with just less than 100 blended learning students pursuing our MSc in Responsible Tourism Management and ten doctoral students.

The ICRT is for Responsible Tourism. Our work focuses on the principles of the Cape Town Declaration on Responsible Tourism in Destinations, we work in originating markets and destinations around the world, to harness tourism to make "better places for people to live in and for people to visit." We work with governments, tour operators and accommodation providers to realise the aspirations of the Responsible Tourism Movement in which we have played a major part since 1997.

Our aspiration is to be a critical friend, raising issues but working together to find solutions, we seek to encourage and enable people to take responsibility for making the changes necessary to make tourism more sustainable. We research the issues around the sustainability of tourism and advocate solutions based on research and scholarly activity. We believe that evidence and clear thinking matters.

The Centre was founded by Harold Goodwin at Greenwich University and it moved with him to Leeds in 2006. Harold was part of the VSO and Tearfund advocacy campaigns which started Responsible Tourism in the UK and worked with the South African government to implement their policy in 2000. Former students have included Justin Frances who is CEO of Responsible Travel.com, Caroline Warburton who runs Wild Scotland and the travel writer Catherine Mack. We have a host of students and former students working in government and sustainability roles in hotels and tour operations around the world, we have alumni in sustainable tourism roles in ABTA, Thomas Cook and TUI. Many are doing work in conservation and consultancy. All of them are taking responsibility and making tourism more sustainable.

Our Masters primarily attracts mid-career professionals who often study the programme whilst continuing their careers in tourism, consultancy, government, conservation, IT, environmental management, law, marketing and a range of other careers. They share a commitment to the values of Responsible Tourism. Our staff are able to work in English, Spanish and German. The Masters is also being provided in India and The Gambia from autumn 2010. We are proud to have Professor Richard Butler, Britain's leading sustainable tourism academic, as our external examiner.

The ICRT has seven core staff, eighteen associates chosen for their complementary expertise, and around a hundred alumni - it has become a significant network with sister organisations in eight countries. Our associates assist us in our ambition to be at the cutting edge of work furthering Responsible Tourism. We have been raising questions about water, travel philanthropy, carbon offsetting and certification for some time, more recently we have begun to raise the issues which arise when the principles of Responsible Tourism are applied to the cruise industry and looking at the issues which arise for people with disabilities.

The ICRT runs with governments around the world an annual International Conference on Responsible Tourism in Destinations, the next is in October 2010 in Oman, in 2011 it will be in Canada and in 2012 in Rio.

In London and Leeds we run regular professional conferences and seminars most recently on responsible cruising and on poverty reduction, others are planned on aviation, hospitality and the organising of excursions which benefit local communities.

Harold Goodwin was part of the Pro-Poor Tourism Partnership which originated work on the tourism and poverty reduction agenda and continues to work on tourism and livelihoods with the United Nations World Tourism Organisation, the International Trade Centre and companies and initiatives in the UK and around the world.

Harold Goodwin chairs the judging panel for the Virgin Holidays Responsible Tourism Awards, the Advisory Panel of the International Tourism Partnership and increasingly works as an advisor; he is Advisor to the World Travel Market on their World Responsible Tourism Day and is currently advising the Ministry of Tourism in Oman on their Responsible Tourism policy.

Xavier Font consults and advises on responsible tourism marketing for VisitEngland and several regional governments and national parks in England and Wales, and also the private sector. He has just conducted a three year monitoring project for the International Finance Corporation on the business impacts of marketing responsible tourism. He enjoys most training companies on market-led responsible change management.

How Responsible Tourism Differs from Sustainable Tourism

Responsible tourism and sustainable tourism have an identical goal, that of sustainable development. The pillars of responsible tourism are therefore the same as those of sustainable tourism - environmental integrity, social justice and maximising local economic benefit. The major difference between the two is that, in responsible tourism, individuals, organisations and businesses are asked to take responsibility for their actions and the impacts of their actions. This shift in emphasis has taken place because not much progress has been made on realising sustainable tourism since the Earth Summit in Rio. This is partly because everyone has been expecting others to behave in a sustainable way. The emphasis on responsibility in responsible tourism means that everyone involved in tourism - government, product owners and operators, transport operators, community services, NGO's and CBO's, tourists, local communities, industry associations - are responsible for achieving the goals of responsible tourism.GITPAC International is the first implementing agency of Responsible Tourism in four destination in kerala for Department of Tourism Government of Kerala.

The Forces that are Driving the Growth in Responsible Tourism

Other than the fact that Responsible Tourism is the right thing to do, the following reasons should motivate tourism destinations businesses to adopt responsible tourism practices.

Planet Panic

Globally, concerns about global warming, destruction of the environment, erosion of cultures and lifestyles, and millions of people still living in poverty, are increasing. The number of initiatives aimed at saving some part of the environment, or improving the living conditions for the world's vulnerable people, increases by the day. This heightened awareness of the earth's crisis is spilling over into the way people behave in their homes, how they spend their money and the way businesses are run. Driven by changing personal ethics, individuals contribute financially or otherwise to environmental and humanitarian initiatives. They are also changing their buying patterns. There is a major upswing in responsible or ethical consumerism in the UK and in other major European markets. In the UK, the market share for ethical products grew by 22% between 1999 and 2004.

Customers Increasingly Demand It

Increasing numbers of consumers are looking at the reputation and responsibility of the companies they buy from; they want to have "guilt free" holidays. This affects their direct purchases from companies in tourism destinations and it influences the choices of source market companies too. UK and other European and Australian companies and increasingly American companies are asking about the responsibility of their suppliers and introducing check lists which rate the sustainability of their practices.

Responsible Tourism Makes Business Sense

A significant, and growing, number of tourists are looking for a better experience, a better quality product. They are looking for experiences which enable them to get closer to the "real" living culture of countries and to experience our diverse natural and cultural heritage. This is a global trend in the established markets as consumer expectations of their holidays change, people are taking more, shorter trips, and they expect to get more from them. In commercial market research UK holidaymakers were asked whether or not they would be more likely to book a holiday with a company if they had a written code to guarantee good working conditions, protect the environment and support charities in the tourist destination. In 1999 45% said yes, when the question was asked again in 2001 52% said yes.

It is a market trend that any tourism business cannot ignore. Responsible Tourism makes business sense because a growing proportion of consumers are looking for a better product. This trend implies that tourism businesses that practice Responsible Tourism will have a powerful competitive advantage over other tourism products.

Objectives of Tourism Development

Tourism Development - Can be defined as the process of providing facilities and services for visitors to a destination in order to gain economic and other benefits

Economic Objects

The economic objectives of tourism development include:

Employment creation Increasing foreign currency earnings Tourist contributions to the multiplier effect - the additional revenue created in an area as a result of tourisum expenditure.

Direct employment - occurs in hotels, airports, airlines, tour operators, travel agents, and tourist offices.

Indirect employment - occurs in industries that serve the travel and tourism industry.

Environmental Objectives

Environmental education - this is usually through visitor centres. this information helps the tourist understand the reasons for conservation and encourages them to respect the environment. Conservation Environments improvements Preservation of wildlife habitats Regeneration - is used to preserve heritage sites.

Socio-cultural Objectives

- Promoting cultural understanding Enhancing the image of an area Creating a national identity
- Partnerships.

Responsible Tourism in Destinations

Shaping Sustainable Spaces into Better Places

We, representatives of inbound and outbound tour operators, emerging entrepreneurs in the tourism industry, national parks, provincial conservation authorities, all spheres of government, tourism professionals, tourism authorities,

NGOs and hotel groups and other tourism stakeholders, from 20 countries in Africa, North and South America, Europe and Asia; having come together in Cape Town to consider the issue of Responsible Tourism in Destinations have agreed this declaration.

Mindful of the debates at the United Nations Commission on Sustainable Development in 1999, which asserted the importance of the economic, social and environment aspects of sustainable development and of the interests of indigenous peoples and local communities in particular.

Recognising the global challenge of reducing social and economic inequalities and reducing poverty, and the importance of New Partnership for Africa's Development (NEPAD) in the process.

Recognising the importance of the World Tourism Organization's Global Code of Ethics, which aims to promote responsible, sustainable and universally accessible tourism and sharing its commitment to equitable, responsible and sustainable world tourism and its STEP initiative with UNCTAD, which seeks to harness sustainable tourism to help eliminate poverty.

Conscious that we are now ten years on from the Rio Earth Summit on Environment and Development, and that the World Summit on Sustainable Development taking place in Johannesburg will put renewed emphasis on sustainability, economic development, and in particular on poverty reduction.

Aware of the World Tourism Organization, World Travel and Tourism Council and the Earth Council's updated Agenda 21 for the Travel and Tourism Industry and the success achieved by a number of businesses, local communities and national and local governments in moving towards sustainability in tourism.

Aware of the work of the UNEP, and the Tourism Industry Report 2002, and work of UNESCO, and other UN agencies, promoting sustainable tourism in partnership with the private sector, NGOs, civil society organisations and government.

Aware of the guidelines for sustainable tourism in vulnerable ecosystems being developed in the framework of the Convention on Biological Diversity.

Conscious of developments in other industries and sectors, and in particular of the growing international demand for ethical business, and the adoption of clear Corporate Social Responsibility (CSR) policies by companies, and the transparent reporting of achievements in meeting CSR objectives in company annual reports.

Recognising that there has been considerable progress in addressing the environmental impacts of tourism, although there is a long way to go to achieve sustainability; and that more limited progress has been made in harnessing tourism for local economic development, for the benefit of communities and indigenous peoples, and in managing the social impacts of tourism.

Endorsing the Global Code of Ethics and the importance of making all forms of tourism sustainable through all stakeholders taking responsibility for creating better forms of tourism and realising these aspirations.

Relishing the diversity of our world's cultures, habitats and species and the wealth of our cultural and natural heritage, as the very basis of tourism, we accept that responsible and sustainable tourism will be achieved in different ways in different places.

Accepting that, in the words of the Global Code of Ethics, an attitude of tolerance and respect for the diversity of religious, philosophical and moral beliefs, are both the foundation and the consequence of responsible tourism.

Recognising that dialogue, partnerships and multi-stakeholder processes - involving government, business and local communities - to make better places for hosts and guests can only be realised at the local level, and that all stakeholders have different, albeit interdependent, responsibilities; tourism can only be managed for sustainability at the destination level.

Conscious of the importance of good governance and political stability in providing the context for responsible tourism in destinations, and recognising that the devolution of decision making power to democratic local government is necessary to build stable partnerships at a local level, and to the empowerment of local communities.

Aware that the management of tourism requires the participation of a broad range of government agencies and particularly at the local destination level.

Recognising that in order to protect the cultural, social and environmental integrity of destinations limits to tourism development are sometimes necessary.

Having, during the Cape Town Conference, examined the South African Guidelines for Responsible Tourism, tested them in a series of field visits, and explored how tourism can be made to work better for local communities, tourists and businesses alike, we recognise their value in helping to shape sustainable tourism in South Africa.

Recognising that one of the strengths of the South African Guidelines for Responsible Tourism is that they were developed through a national consultative process, and that they reflect the priorities and aspirations of the South African people.

Recognising that Responsible Tourism takes many forms, that different destinations and stakeholders will have different priorities, and that local policies and guidelines will need to be developed through multi-stakeholder processes to develop responsible tourism in destinations.

Having the following characteristics, Responsible Tourism:

- minimises negative economic, environmental, and social impacts;
- generates greater economic benefits for local people and enhances the well-being of host communities, improves working conditions and access to the industry;
- involves local people in decisions that affect their lives and life chances;

- makes positive contributions to the conservation of natural and cultural heritage, to the maintenance of the world's diversity;
- provides more enjoyable experiences for tourists through more meaningful connections with local people, and a greater understanding of local cultural, social and environmental issues;
- provides access for physically challenged people; and
- is culturally sensitive, engenders respect between tourists and hosts, and builds local pride and confidence

We call upon countries, multilateral agencies, destinations and enterprises to develop similar practical guidelines and to encourage planning authorities, tourism businesses, tourists and local communities - to take responsibility for achieving sustainable tourism, and to create better places for people to live in and for people to visit.

We urge multilateral agencies responsible for development strategies to include sustainable responsible tourism in their outcomes.

Determined to make tourism more sustainable, and accepting that it is the responsibility of all stakeholders in tourism to achieve more sustainable forms of tourism, we commit ourselves to pursue the principles of Responsible Tourism.

Convinced that it is primarily in the destinations, the places that tourists visit, where tourism enterprises conduct their business and where local communities and tourists and the tourism industry interact, that the economic, social and environmental impacts of tourism need to be managed responsibly, to maximise positive impacts and minimise negative ones. We undertake to work in concrete ways in destinations to achieve better forms of tourism and to work with other stakeholders in destinations. We commit to build the capacity of all stakeholders in order to ensure that they can secure an effective voice in decision making. We uphold the guiding principles for Responsible Tourism which were identified:

Guiding Principles for Economic Responsibility

- Assess economic impacts before developing tourism and exercise preference for those forms of development that benefit local communities and minimise negative impacts on local livelihoods (for example through loss of access to resources), recognising that tourism may not always be the most appropriate form of local economic development
- Maximise local economic benefits by increasing linkages and reducing leakages, by ensuring that communities are involved in, and benefit from, tourism. Wherever possible use tourism to assist in poverty reduction by adopting pro-poor strategies
- Develop quality products that reflect, complement, and enhance the destination
- Market tourism in ways which reflect the natural, cultural and social integrity of the destination, and which encourage appropriate forms of tourism
- Adopt equitable business practises, pay and charge fair prices, and build partnerships in ways in which risk is minimised and shared, and recruit and employ staff recognising international labour standards
- Provide appropriate and sufficient support to small, medium and micro enterprises to ensure tourism-related enterprises thrive and are sustainable

Guiding Principles for Social Responsibility

- Actively involve the local community in planning and decision-making and provide capacity building to make this a reality
- Assess social impacts throughout the life cycle of the operation - including the planning and design phases

of projects - in order to minimise negative impacts and maximise positive ones

- Endeavour to make tourism an inclusive social experience and to ensure that there is access for all, in particular vulnerable and disadvantaged communities and individuals
- Combat the sexual exploitation of human beings, particularly the exploitation of children
- Be sensitive to the host culture, maintaining and encouraging social and cultural diversity
- Endeavour to ensure that tourism contributes to improvements in health and education

Guiding Principles for Environmental Responsibility

- Assess environmental impacts throughout the life cycle of tourist establishments and operations - including the planning and design phase - and ensure that negative impacts are reduced to the minimum and maximising positive ones
- Use resources sustainably, and reduce waste and over-consumption
- Manage natural diversity sustainably, and where appropriate restore it; and consider the volume and type of tourism that the environment can support, and respect the integrity of vulnerable ecosystems and protected areas
- Promote education and awareness for sustainable development - for all stakeholders
- Raise the capacity of all stakeholders and ensure that best practice is followed, for this purpose consult with environmental and conservation experts

We recognise that this list is not exhaustive and that multi-stakeholder groups in diverse destinations should adapt these principles to reflect their own culture and environment.

Responsible tourism seeks to maximise positive impacts and to minimise negative ones. Compliance with all relevant international and national standards, laws and regulations is assumed. Responsibility, and the market advantage that can go with it, is about doing more than the minimum.

We recognise that the transparent and auditable reporting of progress towards achieving responsible tourism targets and benchmarking, is essential to the integrity and credibility of our work, to the ability of all stakeholders to assess progress, and to enable consumers to exercise effective choice.

We commit to making our contribution to move towards a more balanced relationship between hosts and guests in destinations, and to create better places for local communities and indigenous peoples; and recognising that this can only be achieved by government, local communities and business cooperating on practical initiatives in destinations.

We call upon tourism enterprises and trade associations in originating markets and in destinations to adopt a responsible approach, to commit to specific responsible practises, and to report progress in a transparent and auditable way, and where appropriate to use this for market advantage. Corporate businesses can assist by providing markets, capacity building, mentoring and micro-financing support for small, medium and micro enterprises.

In order to implement the guiding principles for economic, social and environmental responsibility, it is necessary to use a portfolio of tools, which will include regulations, incentives, and multi-stakeholder participatory strategies. Changes in the market encouraged by consumer campaigns and new marketing initiatives also contribute to market driven change.

Local authorities have a central role to play in achieving responsible tourism through commitment to supportive policy frameworks and adequate funding. We call upon local authorities and tourism administrations to develop - through multi-stakeholder processes - destination management strategies and responsible tourism guidelines to create better places for host communities and the tourists who visit. Local Agenda 21 programs, with their participatory and monitoring processes, are particularly useful.

We call upon the media to exercise responsibility in the way in which they portray tourism destinations, to avoid raising false expectations and to provide balanced and fair reporting.

We all have a responsibility to make a difference by the way we act.

CHAPTER-5

ADVENTURE LIFE CONSERVATION THROUGH TRAVEL

Adventure Life is an adventure travel company that provides private and small-group tours in Latin America and small-ship cruises throughout the world. They offer over 100 different itineraries in South America and Central America, and hundreds of small-ship cruises to less conventional destinations such as Africa, the Arctic, Antarctica and Alaska. Their focus is nature, cultural, and active travel and they apply ecotourism principles to their tour and cruise programs. Most trips have a maximum group size of 12, and the average size is 8. Since their founding in 1999, over 16,000 clients have traveled with the company. Adventure Life is registered in the State of Montana as ALJ, Inc., and they do business as Adventure Life Journeys and Adventure Life VOYAGES.

Adventure Life was founded by Brian Morgan in 1999. Morgan was working as a consultant in Quito for CARE in the late 1990s, but decided to return home to Montana. While applying for jobs in Montana, Morgan planned a group tour back to Ecuador and promoted it locally. This experience made him recognize that guided tours were a service in demand, and a niche industry that his own travel experiences and Ecuadorian connections had prepared him to explore further.

Adventure Life launched in February 1999 with Spanish language study-trips, internships, and tours to Peru and Ecuador. Office is initially located in Havre, Montana. Morgan hired first staff member. First year of business, Adventure Life has fewer than 100 travelers.

Starting in 2000, The Company decided to focus on offering tours only, and no longer provides Spanish language study-trips, or internships. Office moves from Havre, and settles in Missoula, Montana. By the end of 2000, company hires 4 full-time staff members. Establishes a partner office in Lima, Peru.

Between 2001-2003, Adventure Life added tours to Bolivia, Costa Rica and Belize, Chile, Argentina, Patagonia and Guatemala. They also Establishes a second partner office in Quito, Ecuador. The company moves from Morgan's home into its first office.In 2005, tours started sending travelers to Antarctica. The next year they added Panama to the list of destinations.

Adventure Life also launched Adventure Life VOYAGES , which provide small-ship cruises throughout the world. During 2007, Adventure Life provides trips for over 3500 travelers. In 2008 they added the Falkland Islands. Company launches an online community forum offering client Trip Journals - system utilizes the services of Google Maps.

Responsible Travel

Adventure Life is an active member of the International Galapagos Tour Operators Association, (IGTOA) . The president of Adventure Life, Brian Morgan, is also currently the president of IGTOA. In Nov. 2006, IGTOA they launched a Galapagos traveler-funding program for island conservation, and Adventure Life was one of the first members to adopt this initiative. A voluntary donation is added to all of Adventure Life's Galapagos travelers' invoices. 40% of this donation goes to IGTOA and 60% goes to the Charles Darwin Foundation. Dollar for dollar, Adventure Life matches these donations with travel vouchers for future trips with their company. As of June

2008, Adventure Life's travelers have raised nearly $40,000 for island conservation.

IGTOA supports program in the Galapagos that include both Conservation and Professional Standards. Conservation funding is for projects that directly impact issues like introduced species, patrol of the park, and scientific research. Professional Standards relates to boat safety; passenger care; training and treatment of captains and crew members; guide training; educating travelers on conservation issues; and other issues relating to health, safety, and the rights and responsibilities of both travelers and tourist industry personnel.

The Charles Darwin Foundation (CDF) has carried out research for the conservation of the Galapagos ecosystem for almost 50 years. They have been a leader in conservation science and the practical application of information gained and lessons learned in Galapagos, and are one the most respected non-profit research organization currently in operation.

The CTTC is a non-profit organization established in 1996 to aid in the survival of Incan textile traditions and to provide support to weaving communities. Working with the Center, Quechua weavers and their families in the region of the former Incan capitol are engaged in skills-building, community networking and market development. By researching and documenting complex styles and techniques of the ancestors, the Center helps to ensure that 2,000 year-old textiles traditions will not be lost to future generations. Adventure Life provides an annual donation to the CTTC, and incorporates visits to the center for all of its Peru itineraries that spend time in the Cusco region.

Conservation Through Travel

Everyone acknowledges the two sides of conservation - ecological and cultural - but little attention is paid to the latter. Adventure Life believes it is critical that local people be made active partners in developing a local tourism industry. Money generated by tourism should stay in the community. This means hiring local guides, staying in locally owned hotels, and using the local transportation infrastructure - issues that have been at the heart of our travel philosophy from the beginning.

Travelers can make another important contribution - information. Material benefits often slip through the hands of the local community. Honest information from travelers from the outside world can help people make informed decisions, empowering them in their own economic development. So join us on a journey of learning and discovery, and share a bit of yourself in a land of warm smiles and open hearts.

A recent survey prepared by the Travel Industry Association of America with the support of the National Geographic Society suggests that more than 55 million American travelers desire travel experiences that "protect and preserve the ecological and cultural environment" of the destinations they visit. An even greater number, 77 million, prefer to learn as much as possible about their destination's customs, geography and culture. To meet these demands something called "community tourism" has developed. Community tourism refers to locally-initiated offerings that preserve the natural and cultural resources of destinations, while producing better livelihoods and higher standards of living for residents. It empowers local people to identify the cultural and natural resources in their midst and convert them into assets that can improve the economic life of their community. In so doing, community tourism becomes the engine for restoring and preserving those irreplaceable resources. This style of tourism falls under the umbrella of low-impact, socially conscious travel widely know as "ecotourism."

Each trip we take creates an opportunity to have either a positive or negative effect on our destination; thankfully, the choice is ours. By spending our tourism dollars responsibly and patronizing outfitters and lodges that practice ecotourism, we send a powerful message. Our habits can encourage others to follow our lead, and challenge the average company to raise the bar when it comes to managing their environmental footprint.

Before you go:

There are conflicting uses of the term ecotourism. Many tour operators use this term for marketing purposes only, appealing to the public's increased awareness of environmental matters. Other tour companies are very careful to construct their itineraries in an eco-friendly way. Each trip you take is an opportunity to make a difference, and by doing some preliminary research you can select an environmentally responsible company whose trips benefit the communities in which they take place.

Here are a list of questions to help you discern if the company you are selecting really is an eco-tour company:

Does the company:

- Build environmental and cultural awareness through education, activities, and pre-departure information?
- Provide direct financial contributions for conservation efforts?
- Minimize impact on the environment and the local culture?
  - Travel in small groups?
  - Train tour guides in "Leave No Trace" ethics?
  - Respect local culture?
  - Look for lodgings that emphasize local traditions?
  - Seek out excursions offered by local or indigenous people?
- Support local businesses and service providers?
  - Use locally owned services - hotels, lodges and transport companies - to ensure that as much revenue as possible stays within, and therefore benefits local communities?
  - Partake of community tourism offerings whenever possible - walking tours, overnight stays, purchases of locally made products?
- Offer site-sensitive accommodations?

- Use hotels that:
  - Conserve natural resources-water, electricity, etc.?
  - Use recycled products?
  - Use non-toxic cleaning products?
  - Use fresh, filtered air in guest rooms rather than recycled air?
  - Reduce water consumption by opting out of frequent changes of towels and bed linens?
  - Reduce electricity consumption by favoring fluorescent or other low-energy lighting?

Be Respectful of Nature

- If possible walk/horse ride/bike only on designated trails. This prevents vegetation damage and erosion. If you have to travel off trail, walk on durable surfaces and have your group spread out so that new trails aren't created.
- Remember you are traveling through the animals' backyard - observe all wildlife from a distance and don't attempt to feed the animals.
- Try not to leave any traces of your visit. This will allow everyone to enjoy such places as nature intended.
- Snorkelers & divers need to practice minimal impact techniques so as to avoid touching corals, and marine life.
- Don't be tempted to collect living or dead items or historically significant souvenirs.

Reduce Waste

- In many developing countries and remote places, waste management facilities are limited or nonexistent and recycling is unheard of. You can help minimize the impact from your visit by selecting products with minimal packaging, using reusable water bottles (like

Nalgene brand), and purchasing drinks in glass bottles as these tend to be reused.

Pack it in, Pack it out

- Do not dump garbage. If you bring it, take it back with you. If you find garbage others have missed or dropped by accident, pick it up.
- When hiking do not bury toilet paper, as animals will often dig it up and spread it all over. Instead pack it out. Carry out all plastic or cotton feminine hygiene products.

Protect Water Systems & Oceans

- Wash yourself and your dishes 200 feet from any water sources and away from campsites
- On extended backcountry trips, don't use soap or shampoo; even biodegradable soap still has an impact on the environment. If you do have to use soap use it 200 feet from any water sources and the smallest amount necessary.

Leave what you Find

- Take only pictures, leave only the lightest of footprints, and bring home only memories.
- Leave the place you're visiting in a natural condition.

Be Considerate of Other Visitors

- Preserve the solitude; respect others by traveling and camping quietly.
- Uphill hikers have the right of way.

Respect Cultural Differences

- Local customs and traditions are often different to our own; take time to learn what behaviors are acceptable and what is not.

- Ask permission before taking photographs of local people - carrying a Polaroid is a good opportunity to make new friends, and many families will never have had a picture of their children.
- Taking the time to learn a few words and phrases in your host's native tongue is always appreciated and is a great introduction to starting an interaction with locals.

Purchasing Power

- Help endangered species - do not buy products that exploit wildlife, cause habitat destruction, or come from endangered species.
- Buy locally made goods.
- Travelers can make another important contribution - information. Material benefits often slip through the hands of the local community. Honest information from travelers from the outside world can help people make informed decisions, empowering them in their own economic development.

Adventure Life's Commitment to Sustainable Travel

Adventure Life specializes in travel to the Galapagos Islands, trips to Ecuador, Machu Picchu, the Inca Trail, the Amazon and Andes, as well as a number of tours to Costa Rica, Belize, Guatemala and Antarctica. Their tours are carefully designed to offer the best of each region, while at the same time ensuring a positive impact on the local culture and environment. This is the spirit of Adventure Life's travel philosophy - sustainable travel.

Company founder, Brian Morgan, explains: "travel entails an invaluable relationship between visitors and hosts. We do our best to try and give back to the places and people that have inspired our company from the very start. Their success is our success. From the very beginning, we introduced a number of self-imposed guidelines to ensure that each

Adventure Life itinerary has a positive impact on the local culture, environment, economy, promoting sustainable tourism." There are a number of things that Adventure Life does as part of their everyday operating standards, such as the use of expert local guides, family-run hotels, and local transportation infrastructures. But it goes far beyond that; Adventure Life also supports non-profits and other organizations that encourage cultural and ecological awareness and conservation.

The company is dedicated to supplying its travelers with the literature, the information and the means to be active participants and advocates of responsible travel. One example is their involvement with the International Galapagos Tour Operators Association (IGTOA). Every time a guest of Adventure Life visits the Galapagos, the company donates a passenger fee to IGTOA, amounting to thousands of dollars each year that are used for scholarships and conservation efforts within the Islands. Adventure Life has also helped founder Morgan to create his own non-profit, the Earth Family Fund, which seeks to involve Adventure Life's travelers in the long-term support of the communities visited during their tours.

Adventure Life's motto is that travel should be unexpected and fascinating. It should awaken questions and encourage answers. This is the company's focus - to make travel easier while also making it important, rewarding, and precious. By taking this approach, Adventure Like makes travel better for all parties involved. And their strategy has proven to be very effective, as they're now one of the largest tour operators in Latin America.

CHAPTER-6

TOURISM AND DEVELOPING WORLD

Tourism is a vital part of the global economy, generating roughly $1 trillion as parts of the developing world increasingly become popular vacation spots. In effect, the tourist industry can help create peace and stability in developing countries by providing jobs, diversifying local economies, promoting cross-cultural awareness, among other benefits. In a new USIP report, "Tourism in the Developing World," authors Raymond Gilpin and Martha Honey recommend how countries can maximize this industry's potential by having a robust regulatory framework, investing in infrastructure and human capital, and reducing crime and corruption. Gilpin and Honey examine India, Kenya and Nigeria as case studies and draw lessons learned for other developing countries to build a thriving tourist industry that will also promote peace.

BENEFICIAL OR EXPLOITATIVE

Every few months, it seems, there is a flurry of passionate and well-intentioned opinions that question the viability of tourism centered on poor villages, arguing that the benefits to be gained are outweighed by the potential for exploitation of poor people. Some of the rhetoric in this ongoing debate has shed more heat than light on the issue, but let's focus on some real, on-the-ground facts and positive impacts.

In Rwanda, tourism is currently the largest foreign-exchange earner. The majority of revenue comes from wealthy safari tourists in Kenya and Tanzania who jet in for 2-3 days to see Rwanda's legendary mountain gorillas. However, Rwandans recognize that more tourism is needed and that each additional day a tourist spends in country translates into jobs and growth. That's why a tourism cooperative and a small private tour operator decided to establish a full-day village tour in Mayange, just an hour south of Kigali.

Just a few years ago, Mayange would not have been an enjoyable tourist spot: it had been at the epicenter of the genocide, was one of the poorest sectors in the country, and frequently faced famine. Infant mortality was high, the health center was scarcely open, there was no paved road link to Kigali, there was minimal agricultural activity, no electricity, and questionable levels of education. Over the past few years, however, the Government of Rwanda, along with the Millennium Villages Project, has worked with the community to transform the situation. Today, Mayange is thriving to such a degree that land prices in the community have more than tripled. Food is abundant, business is springing up, schools are dramatically improved, and mortality rates have dropped substantially.

That's why the people of Mayange decided their story was one worth telling. The tour they designed focuses on the genocide sites down the road in Nyamata and the environmental, educational, agricultural, business and civil accomplishments cultivated by the community through work with the Millennium Villages project. Tours bring visitors to the villages, where farmers talk to them about agriculture; weavers show off their skills and sell their wares; dancers perform local pieces; and myriad others in the community benefit from interacting with them.

Within Mayange, there are several community cooperatives (including weaving, agriculture, theatre, and others), all of which benefit financially from the visits of interested tourists who want to know more about the community. The community initially decided to partner with a private company to arrange these tours; today, two private companies offer the tour. Community leaders consider tourism as a means of providing not only financial benefits to themselves, but to promote cross-cultural learning and understanding.

The tourism cooperative leaders insisted on a set of ground rules to encourage the community to view the tourists as a source of wealth creation, not of charity. One of their rules - which has actually garnered a surprising amount of publicity - requests that tourists give out no candy, toys, or food (many outside observers incorrectly concluded that this rule was foisted on the community by outside forces). The community, the district, and national government consider handouts to be part of a cycle of behavior that leads rapidly to dependency.

It's a fair question to ask if all community members benefit from these tours. Community members love the tour, enjoy the visitors, and are proud to show off their accomplishments. At the end of each tour, which cost about $60 per visitor, 70% of the money collected is given back to the community and distributed among those who participate directly in the tour. With a large number of visiting tourists and a significant number of tours, this is a major injection of capital into the local economy. To maintain fairness, the cooperative makes sure that the farmers, dancers and other cooperative members who meet with tourists (and thus get the largest share of the profits) rotate with each tour. Everyone benefits.

The life of Mukasinadere, a member of a weaving cooperative, has been completely changed by the tours. Working as a weaver and selling baskets to tourists, she is now able to pay for her family's basic needs. Quite simply, she and her kids now have enough food to eat, but she is also able to buy clothes for her children, including school uniforms. This last piece is crucial - without these uniforms, her children would not be able to attend school.

The weavers, all of whom are women, have benefited from the tours in a way they have never been able to before. In the past in this community, women were completely dependent on their husbands and their meager earnings from subsistence agriculture for money. Now, their weaving cooperatives allow them to earn and spend money independently - a huge step toward a more equitable distribution of wealth and autonomy in the community. Another example of how the tours are helping make gender equality a reality is with the women who provide meals for tourists. This enterprise has been so profitable, and the women have earned so much, the cooperative has invested over $10,000 in a local restaurant, which is slated to open soon.

The bottom line: tourism in Rwanda helps eradicate poverty and hunger. It makes it possible for more children to go to school. It helps bridge the divide between cultures, not deepen it. It leads to more gender equality, not more exploitation. Most importantly, it creates real, sustainable prosperity that is not dependent on charity.

Tourism in general and the Mayange tours in particular are good for economic development. With low barriers to entry, tourism is a great way for developing countries to employ people while increasing their GDP. Tourism as envisioned and initiated by Rwandans should be promoted, not disparaged.

Tourism Educational and Training Policies in Developing Countries

For most Caribbean countries, and some developing nations in other regions, tourism constitutes the most heavily favored vehicle for economic development. One of the characteristics of island tourism destinations, particularly in the developing world, is their heavy reliance on a limited range of economic sectors, generally dominated by tourism. More and more countries and regions increasingly court the vast international tourist market as other economic options decline. Tourism is a growing international business with increasing revenues.1 Some commentators have justifiably raised important concerns about the negative impacts of tourism on developing countries. Destinations that have the most to gain from tourism, might also be the most vulnerable to its negative aspects.2 Tourism does, however, provide much needed foreign exchange for countries with limited economic bases. Even the most cautious analyses do not suggest eliminating tourism completely. Carefully designed, implemented and managed tourism policies can make a substantial contribution to national economic development.

Defining and implementing a realistic and appropriate tourism policy, whether on the local, national or regional level, requires careful long-term planning. In addition to setting achievable goals, policy makers must also make decisions about educating and training nationals to implement the stated objectives. Education and training are critical aspects of tourism policy formation and enactment. Unfortunately, the issues of education and training, arguably the most critical aspect of formulating and implementing tourism policy, have been sorely neglected in the literature on tourism development and at the level of policy decision making.

This article examines the issue of tourism policy, with a particular emphasis on education and training, in one of the best-known tourist destinations in the world, the Cayman Islands in the Caribbean. The regional economy of the Caribbean basin increasing relies on tourism, especially from the United States, one of the largest tourist generating markets in the world. The Cayman Islands, currently engaged in a massive advertising campaign overseas, is one of the leaders in the region in attracting tourists. It is also the most economically developed location in the region with a per capita income of CI$24,300.3 Much of the Caymans' economic strength can be directly linked to tourism. Simultaneously, the Caymanian tourist industry, especially in the areas of policy formulation and education, does have serious weaknesses that will only be exacerbated as the industry expands. A case study of the government's tourism and related education and training policies, a neglected area of analysis, can shed considerable light on a critical ingredient of that nation's, and the region's, economy. It can also offer guidelines for other developing countries and regions in formulating tourism and education policies.

Tourism Policy Options

Attracting tourists from overseas and developing a tourist industry requires the creation and operation of quality service. One approach to achieving and sustaining quality service and its resulting tourism development consists of the enactment of a tourism policy that deals with human resources development, primarily education and training. The aim of tourism education in developing countries should be the better functioning of the tourism sector and the destination at large. Policy and education are inextricably linked, and essential for maintaining the tourism sector in a developing country.

Tourism policy's primary purpose should be to integrate the economic, political, cultural, intellectual and environmental benefits of tourism to insure that the global quality of life of people, destinations and countries can be improved while creating a basis for peace and prosperity. Tourism policy operates at the individual, business-related, local, national and transnational levels. In-house training, company health facilities and other enhanced benefit packages are examples of individual business-related facilities. Local initiatives are seen through collective employer actions, resulting from industry, organization or public agency-sponsored actions. These actions can range from self-help provisions, local private investments or governmental actions which come about through private sector persuasions. In terms of a national initiative, coordinating manpower and skills planning within tourism is an essential forerunner of more localized, specifically targeted initiatives. Regional initiatives are very similar to national initiatives but transcend national boundaries. For example, the Caribbean Hotel Association provides specialist training on a regional basis. National policies on tourism in developing countries, especially in the Caribbean, are usually the domain of the state, whereas in more developed countries, private entrepeneurs often dominate policy formation and enactment. In most developing countries, owing to the small size of the private sector and the shortage of funds, the government necessarily takes on the role of entrepeneur. Frequently, this is in response to proposed private foreign investment. The aims of the private sector, more often than not, oppose those of the public sector. Private sector investment criteria hinge upon profitability. The state, on the other hand, must take into account non-economic ramifications as well. Without governmental involvement, short-term developments can foster long-term problems. Governments in the developing world generally have the responsibility of formulating and enforcing tourism policy.

There are two policy options normally followed in developing countries: the status quo option, and the pro-active option. The former is highlighted where policies are designed to keep the system already in place working. This option emphasizes development planning, with funding agencies continuing to concentrate resources on this goal. The focus remains on preparing consistent, logical and integrated plans suited to the situations happening in the country. Implementation policies and procedures receive limited attention. Problems that arise receive a reactive solution in the post-plan period. The pro-active scenario concerns anticipating negative changes that might and can occur, as well as putting policies in place that prevent or mitigate these changes from occuring. In this instance, funding agencies devote more time to post-planning and audit responses. Experts scrutinize the plans, and measure post-plan achievements. Efforts are made to identify the main weaknesses in the implementation process, with the resulting information used to prepare guidelines for future planning exercises.

Caribbean countries, like many other developing countries with a functioning or potential tourism sector, cannot afford to neglect anticipated negative changes that can and do occur with tourism. Their economic dependence on tourism as their primary or even secondary revenue earner makes it imperative that they understand the negative effects that can take place, and prepare for them. Lack of preparation can spell unwanted hardship.

The current emphasis in developing countries, particularly in the Caribbean, centers on the pro-active option for tourism policy. The Caribbean Tourism Organization has embraced this option as evidenced in the following quote by an official:

"The Caribbean needs to do the necessary research as to its manpower needs for the industry, and to put in place short, medium, and long-term plans to address them. In the meantime there is a need for an enlightened policy that facilitates the entry of extra-Caribbean expertise. This policy should also seek to insure that foreign expertise is given the mandate for training Caribbean counterparts."

Further support for a pro-active government policy, dealing specifically with the areas of education and training, can be found in this quote: "Recognition of the value of human resources itself is not enough. A regulatory framework which seeks to ensure the inclusion of the host population in the tourism industry to the fullest extent possible is essential to operationalize this recognition to the highest level. The areas of immigration and education provide good examples."

Baum noted that in terms of education and training for the industry, tourism policy must address two main issues. A strong sense of local responsibility and civic-mindedness is required from employers within the tourism industry to overcome personnal poaching and to facilitate cooperative local tourism industry image development and training intiatives. The major players holding responsibility for the recruitment and training initiatives of the smaller players is a worthwhile model. Additionally, education and training program design should give close attention to the local needs of the various sectors in the industry. There should be systematic research and close liaison and consultation.

Tom Riegbert, from the Organization of American States (OAS), proposed ten policy options for Latin American and

Caribbean countries? These options included the creation of jobs, and the provision of education and training in the tourism sector. He noted the importance of the occupational upgrading of jobs to higher skills, more responsibility and increased controls by nationals. He also expressed concern that qualified human resources were necessary to sustain the development of the tourism sector. The need for more tourism industry skills has justifiably become a particular source of policy concem for Caribbean governments, even those with mature tourism industries, such as the Bahamas and Jamaica. In the Caribbean region, the present policy concern is to integrate tourism education and training throughout the school system. This has worked well in the Bahamas and Barbados. Governments also seek to improve the direct vocational and professional training in schools at the tertiary level, and to offer short courses and seminars in the field.

The Disadvantages of Tourism in Developing Countries

Investing in infrastructure and marketing for tourism is often considered a good strategy for boosting a nation's economy. However, recent debates have arisen concerning the actual effect tourism has within developing countries, and to what extent it helps those most in need of financial assistance.

Leakages in the Tourism Sector-The major drawback to earnings from tourism occurs because of "leakages" - tourism industry earnings that accrue outside the host country. Leakages occur because a sizable percentage of tourism infrastructure is usually foreign-owned and operated. A paper by Blake and Arbache estimates that 55% to 75% of tourism spending "leaks back to developed countries."

Bhatia published a recent paper, "Tourist Development: Principles and Practice", which provides a more detailed account of leakages, showing that they occur primarily in three ways:

- Some tourism employment may be given to foreign workers, thus part of the jobs and income from tourism accrues to them.

- Indirect and direct taxation of tourist activities may result in revenue that is not reinvested in the host area.
- Tourism earnings, which are mostly received in foreign exchange, may be spent on imports or on debts to foreign governments, thus providing no net benefit to the domestic economy and population.

The Crowding Out Potential of Tourism-Other economists believe that an expansion of the tourist sector can "crowd out" other industries. This leads to a lower demand for traditional exports and import competing industries within the economy.

The "crowding out" conclusion is based on the theory that tourism causes a direct increase in demand in non-tradable sectors (hotels, resorts, restaurants, domestic transportation services). This leads to an increase in prices for those services, which in turn attract resources from other sectors of the economy (under the law of one price assumption), leading to a contraction of tradable sectors. Because of this contraction, exports fall while imports rise.

Unequal Gains: The Poor and the Rich-Wattanakuljarus' study of tourism in Thailand also found that tourism does not substantially benefit the country's poor, and thus cannot be used as a pro-poor development strategy. Though the general equilibrium model he used shows that all income classes obtain some benefit from tourism, the benefits are concentrated in high income and non-agricultural households. So tourism-oriented development may cause inequality to increase due to this disproportionate spread of economic gains.

Exogenous Shocks-The study additionally indicates that tourism is vulnerable to what economists term "exogenous shocks in demand" (caused by factors such as natural disasters, global terrorists incidents, disease outbreaks, etc.), that cannot be controlled by domestic macroeconomic policy.

Such shocks can lead to harmful effects for a country that exhibits over-reliance on the tourist sector in the event of a negative exogenous shock; the tourist economy will slump and there is no policy tool to provide immediate remediation in this sector.

Poor Employment Opportunities-Lastly, the employment created by the tourist sector may disadvantage local poor populations, as it is often seasonal, low-paying, and exploitative. Such employment creates little opportunity for economic advancement and improved quality of life.

Tourism can still be an engine for economic growth, but it has to be implemented appropriately by a stable government. The idea of tourism itself as a path to progress for the poor is not flawed, but the above possible negative effects must be considered and controlled.

CHAPTER-7

RESPONSIBLE TOUR OPERATORS

Green tourism and responsible travel are key concerns for AITO and its members. Each potential member's sustainable tourism credentials are examined before they may join, to ensure sustainability and that local cultures and the environment are treated with the utmost care and respect. AITO members recognise that the destinations where they provide holidays are the life blood of the industry. and that they need to protect them with a responsible travel and sustainable tourism policy. AITO is the first tourism industry association to incorporate into its business charter a commitment to Responsible travel and green tourism. Sustainable travel guidelines for its members based upon 5 key objectives:

- To protect the environment - its flora, fauna and landscapes
- To respect local cultures - traditions, religions and built heritage
- To benefit local communities - both economically and socially
- To conserve natural resources - from office to destination
- To minimise pollution - through noise, waste disposal and congestion

Responsible tourism is about making a positive difference when we travel:

- ❖ Enjoying ourselves and taking responsibility for our actions - respecting local cultures and the natural environment
- ❖ Giving fair economic returns to local people - helping to spread the benefit of our visit to those who need it most
- ❖ Recognising that water and energy are precious resources that we need to use carefully.
- ❖ Protecting endangered wildlife and preserving the natural and cultural heritage of the places we visit for the future enjoyment of visitors and the people who live there.

Tour Operators

Members of the Federation of Tour Operators are becoming increasingly aware of the socio-cultural, economic and environmental impacts of their products and services. In 2003, they formed a Responsible Tourism Committee and are developing a series of initiatives to assist tour operators to integrate responsible tourism practices into their core business.

There are an increasing number of tour operators who are marketing their products as 'ecotourism', 'cultural tours', and 'reality tours'. Because these terms mean different things to different people, we have left out the labels and developed some criteria. You can use this checklist to evaluate tour operators and compare travel programs.

Operations

- ❖ Environmental Friendly
- ❖ Company has program to reduce, reuse, and recycle.
- ❖ Recycled content paper used.
- ❖ Conservation of materials (size and volume of promotional materials minimized).
- ❖ Economic Benefits
- ❖ Fairness in the work place.

- Programs that give back to the communities in which they operate.
- Guides/staff reflect ethnic and gender diversity.
- Cultural Sensitivity
- Promotional copy conveys respect and dignity to all people, and is non-voyeuristic.

Programs

- Environmental Friendly
- Transport is efficient/sustainable: use non-motorized transportation or high occupancy vehicles as the primary mode of travel.
- Practices of program are low-impact; life-style and program activities.
- Economic Benefits
- Locally owned businesses are patronized (i.e. not foreign owned hotel chains).
- Locally produced products are consumed (i.e. not imported foodstuffs).
- Purchases made from traditional producers (i.e. artisans and craftspeople)
- Traditional enterprises are encouraged, (i.e. hotels and restaurants that serve local community).
- Bargaining is appreciated in its social role, not as competition.
- Cultural Sensitivity
- Program structure reduces barriers between citizens and visitors.
- Cross-cultural interaction is for more than food, fashion, festivals and photo opportunities.
- Program objectives are qualitative not quantitative.
- Activities are within the moral and ethical standards of the area.

- Appropriate dress for visitors is encouraged.
- Departures on any one itinerary are limited (i.e. less than 1 per month).

Guides/Staff

- Cultural Sensitivity
- Have a background and knowledge of the culture.
- Actions (greeting, transactions) are respectful of the people and their culture.
- Language is respectful of the people and their way of life.
- Dress reflects the traditional values of the community (not necessarily the value, or lack thereof, of the visitors or Hollywood.)
- Photography and video are discouraged where inappropriate.
- Environmental Friendly
- Set an example of respecting the environment.
- Economic Benefits

ADVENTURE ALTERNATIVE

Offers trekking, teaching and medical electives, mountaineering expeditions and safaris, to various countries. "We emphasize pro-poor tourism, putting profits back into local communities and promoting long- term employment in developing countries." The company has offices in Belfast (HQ), Nairobi, Moshi, Moscow and Kathmandu and is linked to and supports the registered charity and NGO Moving Mountains which works in Nepal, Niger and Kenya. Ethical Tour Operators Group member.

Baobab Travel

BAOBAB is a specialist eco-tour operator offering trips mainly to Africa. Destinations include Malawi, Mozambique,

South Africa, Tanzania and Zambia as well as Egypt/Sinai and Jordan. They can provide themed trips from scuba-diving to wildlife safaris and yoga retreats. Ethical Tour Operators Group member.

Cazenove and Lloyd

Based in London this firm describes itself as "destination experts" and focuses on the luxury end of the market with tailor made trips to Latin America, Africa, and Indian Ocean and India. Ethical Tour Operators Group member.

Dragoman Overland

Runs truck-based adventure travel trips with exotic destinations and authentic experiences throughout the world. It has a responsible tourism policy and a strong commitment to local community projects and says at least 55% of passengers' money stays in the destination country to benefit its hosts. Winner of the AITO Responsible Tourism Company of the Year award in 2006.

Eurocamp

Eurocamp calls itself the market-leader in self-catering holidays to Europe, offering the widest choice of camping options in over 180 parcs in 9 countries with facilities for couples and families and activities ranging from canoeing, cycling, horse riding, windsurfing and diving to simply playing in the pools and water features. Its Green Team aims to protect the environment, conserve natural resources and minimise pollution and parent company Holidaybreak has received the prestigious AITO 5-star award for responsible tourism.

Expert Africa

Formerly called Sunvil Africa this company offers safaris and trips to the southern part of the continent. Its staff are experts who spend at least a month there every year. The website includes details of its commitment to responsible travel. Ethical Tour Operators Group member.

Explore Worldwide

Part of the international HolidayBreak group, this Hampshire based adventure travel firm was founded in 1981 and now operates over 300 trips ranging from walking and trekking to cycling, family holidays and short breaks. Travelmole (the online community for the travel and tourism industry) named Explore the best responsible tourism website in 2006. Ethical Tour Operators Group member.

First Choice

Part of the leading international TUI Travel group, First Choice launched its brand new online Greener Holidays brochure in April 2009. Its award winning airline is changing the way it flies to reduce carbon emissions and all the hotels featured have been recognised for doing their bit to be more sustainable by reducing energy and water usage, sourcing locally produced food and making sure their employees have fair working conditions. The best performing hotels are given a bronze, silver or gold Travelife award.

Gane and Marshall

This small specialist London company with a strong interest in ethical and environmental issues provides tailor made itineraries to southern and eastern Africa, South America, and the Indian Ocean ranging from safaris to beach holidays and honeymoons. Ethical Tour Operators Group member.

G.A.P. Adventures

Calling themselves "the great adventure people" this company has specialised in sustainable travel since 1990 with a focus on cultural journeys and wildlife encounters. Its commitment to socially conscious, grassroots style travel has earned numerous ecotourism awards. It offers a wide selection of over 1250 small group adventure tours, family vacations, and small ship cruises in 100 countries on every continent. Groups typically comprise people aged 18 - 80 and trips can last from a few days or a couple of weeks to six months.

Haven Holidays

Haven Holidays owns and operates 35 award-winning family holiday parks throughout England, Scotland and Wales - close to some of Britain's most beautiful beaches and brightest resorts. Accommodation ranges from caravans, chalets, apartments, tents and yurts. There are pools, kids clubs, sports facilities, and family entertainment. Environmental concerns are taken seriously and measures include water conservation, recycling and reducing energy consumption. Four Parks have prestigious Green Tourism Business Scheme awards, one with Gold status.

The Imaginative Traveller

Provides more than 300 small group tours and treks in a variety of styles and comfort levels. These are experience led rather than activity based going to the heart of a destination, getting off the tourist trail, meeting the locals, and spending time with them in their natural environment. Destinations include Africa, Antarctica, Asia, Central and South America, Central Asia, Europe, the Middle East and South East Asia. It says it has been committed to sustainable tourism since its launch in 1991 with local partnerships, suppliers and staff.

Intrepid Travel

The company has over 300 different small group adventure trips in over 50 different destinations in Europe, Asia, Africa, Latin America, North America, the Middle East, Antarctica and Australia, and many different styles of travel. Notable for its responsible tourism policy, its aim is that travellers become a part of country and not just tourists looking in. It has submitted itself to rigorous external audit and established the Intrepid Foundation to aid local causes. Winner in the tour operator category of the 2006 Virgin Holidays Responsible Tourism Awards.

KE Adventure Travel

Specialises in trekking and climbing holidays and stresses its good treatment of local staff, respect for indigenous cultures and aim to make a positive contribution wherever it goes. It offers exciting experiences in mountain ranges in over 40 countries. Winner of the AITO Responsible Tourism Company of the Year award in 2007.

Keycamp Holidays

Mobile home and camping holidays on over 100 sites, in 7 European countries. They're ideal for all age groups from families (with children's clubs for tots to teenagers) or couples seeking an activity holiday - from scuba diving to sailing, cycling to horse riding, windsurfing to canoeing. The firm's environmentally friendly practices have been recognized with the Five Star Award for Responsible Tourism by AITO.

Kuoni

Award winning tour operator specialising in long haul and tailor made holidays to hundreds of exotic destinations worldwide. Its selection of experiences includes exploring, well-being, activity, luxury beach retreats and family friendly holidays. It says it is committed to sustainable tourism and has launched over 30 social, community and environmental projects. In early 2009 it signed up to the Travelife system and will now assess all the hotels it features for sustainability.

Neilson Active Holidays

Activity holidays for adventure seeking solo travellers, groups, and families in beautiful locations year-round. Including skiing, snowboarding, dinghy sailing, wakeboarding, waterskiing, windsurfing, tennis, mountain biking, yachting, scuba diving and kite surfing. It has an ethical travel policy and aims to lower the use of non-renewable resources and implement the Three R's where possible, by Reducing, Re-using and Recycling.

Parkdean Holidays

Operates 24 Holiday Parks in the UK. Accommodation ranges from caravan holiday homes, lodges, apartments and chalets, available for short breaks and longer holidays throughout the year. Caravan and camping pitches are also available at many locations. 12 holiday parks have been given the David Bellamy Conservation gold award for protecting the environment, 10 have silver awards and 1 bronze.

Radical Travel

Radical Travel offers budget trips for 18-35 year olds. These include Shamrocker Adventures: cheap, exciting and fun budget tours of Ireland in midi-coaches; Busabout Explorer: flexible travel for backpackers and independent travellers with a hop-on hop-off network covering 30 destinations in 10 European countries; Busabout Adventures: a collection of trips around Europe and North Africa ranging from sailing in Croatia to truck trips round Morocco; and Haggis Adventures: tours in England, Scotland and Wales - and the first ever tour operator in Scotland to receive a Green Tourism Business Scheme environmental award.

Rainbow Tours

Rainbow Tours is a specialist travel company based in London providing tailor-made holidays to Africa and the Indian Ocean. It creates individual safaris, honeymoons, bush and beach holidays, preferring owner-run accommodation in unusual and interesting destinations. It includes lodges certified by FTTSA, the South African fair trade in tourism body, and says it aims "to turn the rhetoric of ecotourism into reality" through its code of practice. Ethical Tour Operators Group member.

Responsible Travel

A renowned online travel directory which claims to have been the first to talk about responsible travel and tourism and the first business dedicated to promoting eco, green or responsible' holidays on one site. It offers thousands of adventure and family holidays, ecotourism and responsible travel from hundreds of tour operators and accommodation providers which it has screened to meet its environmental, social and economic criteria and explains how each holiday actually makes a difference. The firm says it has arranged travel for over 25,000 clients since 2001. You can't book directly online: you have to send your trip enquiry using their online form and the tour operator calls you back. A co-sponsor of the Responsible Tourism Awards.

Simply Tanzania

The company provides holiday experiences taking in the wildlife and scenic delights of this East African country away from the regular tourist routes as well as giving visitors the chance to meet local people and to gain some understanding of the culture and development issues. Its website says it supports sustainable tourism where possible using locally owned and run tour companies, hotels and lodges.

The Adventure Travel Company

Runs over 230 exciting small group trips to every continent including family and teenage adventures, wildlife encounters, treks, and cultural and activity holidays. Top destinations include Jordan, Nepal, China, Namibia, Brazil, Italy, Botswana, Mexico and New Zealand. It has a responsible tourism policy and over half the trips support a local project, for instance a school in India or a community centre in Tanzania through its Adventure Company Foundation funded by the company and clients' voluntary donations. It also donates a small sum per passenger to offset carbon emissions.

The Co-operative Travel

The UK's largest independent travel agent and part of the world's largest consumer co-operative with strong values and principles on ethics and sustainability. According to a 2008 NOP survey the group is viewed as the most ethical brand in the UK. A full member of ABTA and ATOL protected it sells holidays worldwide from all the top travel companies.

Thomas Cook

The UK's oldest tour operator, established for over 160 years and still inspired by its founder's values. The company has a huge choice of holidays to destinations near and far and says its mission is to perfect the personal leisure experience and to manage its activities in a morally and socially responsible manner. It supports the Travel Foundation's Make Travel Greener campaign and the Travelife awards scheme. It also now offers web chat assistance to customers booking online.

Tribes Travel

Describing itself as "the Fair Trade Travel company", it offers high quality tailor made holidays which benefit local people, wildlife and the environment. It offers holidays in 14 countries worldwide and activities including bird watching, safaris, trekking, cultural or just lazing on a beach. Tribes is based in Suffolk and was the First Choice Responsible Tourism Awards winner in 2005. Ethical Tour Operators Group member.

Upland Escapes

Specialises in independent or small group walking holidays in traditional hamlets, villages and towns, in spectacular undiscovered upland scenery in Europe. In 2007 Upland Escapes won Travel Trade Gazette's "Scream if You're Green" Travel Award, and in November 2008, was highly commended by the Virgin Holidays Responsible Tourism Awards in the Best in a Mountain Environment category for helping to protect mountain village lifestyles.

Wilderness Scotland

This firm runs guided walking, sailing and adventure holidays throughout the highlands and islands of Scotland. Its website features detailed descriptions of its responsible tourism policy and how it puts this into practice. Highly commended at the Respnsible Tourism Awards, 2006.

Tour Operators Role

The dramatic growth of tourist traffic to the Mediterranean countries of Europe is a principal feature of the history of mass tourism in the last forty years. A major contributing factor in this growth of air travel holiday tourism has been the development of 'inclusive tour', a method of packaging a holiday. The idea of buying a package of travel, accommodation and perhaps some ancillary services such as entertainment etc., became established in Western Europe in the 1960s. Essentially an 'inclusive tour' is a package of transport and accommodation and perhaps some other service which is sold as a single holiday for an all inclusive price. This inclusive price is usually significantly lower than could be obtained by conventional methods of booking transport and accommodation separately from individual hotel and transport tariffs. The principal feature of the inclusive tour is that the tourist may buy, for a single price, a holiday which is much cheaper than would be possible for the holiday maker if he bought the components of his holiday separately and directly from individual hotels and from transport companies or from a retail travel agent.

The chief functionary or the principal in this system is the tour operator. It is the tour operator who buys aircraft seats and hotel beds and certain other facilities such as surface transport or entertainment and makes up the package. Historically, the tour operator has mostly emerged from retail travel agency. However, today a clear distinction must be made between tour operator and a travel agent. The latter, the retail travel agent, undertakes to sell the travel services of his principal, who will be airline companies and other transport undertakings, hotel groups, shipping lines and the providers of such ancillary services as traveller's cheques, etc. Unlike the travel agent who is the retailer of the tourism product, the tour operator is a manufacturer of a tourism product. He plans, organises and sells tours. The tour operator makes all the necessary arrangements - transport, accommodation, sight-seeing, insurance, entertainment and other matters and sells this package for an all-inclusive price. A package tour is designed to fit a particular group of travellers. These may be special interest tours, i.e., mountain tours and can be escorted. Escorted tour normally includes transportation, meals, sightseeing, accommodation, guide services, etc. It is the escort or the group leader who is responsible for maintaining the schedule of the tour and for looking after all the arrangements.

Group Inclusive Tour (GIT) : This is the most popular form of tour in this category where people travel in groups of 15 or more persons. These tours are available for any destination. The terms and conditions for group inclusive tours are laid down by IATA. The escort for such groups normally travels free as the airline provides him with free passage and accommodation. "Foreign Inclusive Tours' (FIT) on the other hand are unescorted package tours. These tours are comparatively more flexible. The traveller can buy a predetermined package with arrangements for sightseeing, hotels and certain meals, where necessary. He does not tour with a group. He can make his own arrangements and programmes according to his liking. The inclusive tour is one of the several devices which enable tourists to enjoy the lower prices.

How does the tour operator manage to sell the package to the traveller at such a low price? The low price of the package holiday or inclusive tour is made possible by reason of the lower unit costs obtainable both for the air travel and for the hotel accommodation. The tour operator enters into long-term contracts for aircraft seats and similar contracts with hotels for booking rooms. By mass-producing holidays in the form of package tours, the tour operators are able to procure substantial discounts from carriers, hoteliers, etc. and offer their package deals at much lower rates. The profits of the tour operators and the success of his operations, however, depend on achieving of very high load factors for the aircraft and very high occupancy rates for the hotel. In this way, unit costs can be maintained sufficiently low to enable the tour operator to offer his package at a price which is often less than the cheapest available fare alone. A breakthrough in the business of tour operation came when airlines recognised that tour operation can fill the empty seats and introduced special fares for use exclusively by tour operators for combining into an inclusive tour.

The tour operator has thus emerged as the true manufacturer of the inclusive tour product packaged, standardised and mass-produced. The tour operator may sell this product directly to the public or through the channels of the retail travel agencies. It can be marketed successfully in the tourist generating countries to a mass market just because it is standardised, packaged and quality controlled. The product is therefore susceptible to the similar marketing techniques that are applied to the marketing of consumer goods.

Socially Responsible Tour Operators

The German Travel Association said that a growing number of tour operators are engaged in CSR in their businesses. A good example was Studiosus, which offers "study trip" holiday packages in cooperation with partners in local destinations. It is more up-market because the vacations tend to be expensive. A two-week vacation to Ethiopia, for example, would cost well over 2,500 euros ($3,400 dollars).

Another organization that offers "alternative" volunteer holiday packages is TravelWorks. It cooperates with local partners in different parts of the world. The company offers travelers a stay with a host family combined with social or environmental work in a local institution.

Nico Siegmund, a young German student teacher who participated in a TravelWork program in Ghana in 2009, was happy with his experience there. But he said he felt that it was too costly. Siegmund's two-month volunteer holiday cost 960 euros without air fare, vaccinations, visa or other travel costs.

Best Practices for Responsible Travel for Tour Operators

Green Travel Socio-cultural best practices: Provides clients with pre-trip socio-cultural information. Seeks culturally authentic attractions and educates clients about local culture while on sites. Actively consults with local community members/stakeholders on shared sustainability issues. Does not jeopardize the provision of basic services to local people nor limits their access to local resources or culturally and spiritually important sites. Respects local cultural lifestyles such as dress and food, and encourages sensitivity in clients to the unique customs of the region.

Green Travel Environmental best practices: Provides clients with pre-trip information on ecological issues and attractions. Demonstrates correct knowledge, and respect for, plant and animal life in day-to-day practices, and educates clients on local ecology where appropriate. Makes monetary contributions to conservation efforts in the region. Makes physical (e.g., tree planting) contributions to conservation efforts in the region. Employs measures to actively minimize impacts on the environment (e.g.,carbon offsets). Uses vehicles with lower emissions; uses transportation wisely to reduce environmental impact. Uses solar, wind, or other alternative energy sources in operations at operator's site and destination's. Actively reduces, reuses and recycles at operator's site and destination's. Uses local and fair-trade goods and services.

Economic best Practices: Employs local people, is equitable in hiring women and local minorities, and pays fair wages, meeting or exceeding the highest local standards. Uses companies that are locally owned/operated. Uses accommodations that have been built using local materials where possible and minimize impact on the environment. Uses sustainable products at tour operator's site and destination's. Implements policies against child labor and commercial sexual exploitation. Promotional materials are accurate and complete and do not promise more than can be reasonably expected by customers. Consistently emphasizes quality over quantity.

Policy and Practice best Practices: Elicits and follows up with feedback from clients during the trip. Elicits and follows up with feedback from clients after the trip. Delivers sustainability information to employees at operator's site and destination's. Requires that employees attain industry certifications where appropriate (e.g., wilderness first-aid). Has a risk management plan. Provides a safe environment for employees and clients at operator's site and destination's. Sets appropriate client carrying capacities in line with the ability of the environment to absorb the tour. Seeks to reform policy and/ or practices in the environments in which it operates when appropriate. Sets organizational mission, vision, and values that have a sustainable orientation. Follows a written code of ethics. Supports green travel sustainability programs in the community. Works to exceed compliance with current applicable regulations while working in concert with broader local, regional, and national policies. Prioritizes areas for continuous sustainability improvement at operator's site and destination's.

Chapter-8

RESPONSIBLE TOURISM ORGANIZATION AND RESOURCES

"Global tourism and travel has certainly changed in the past decade. Choices regarding security, safety, health, and the environment have greatly impacted our travel choices. On the other hand, we now have amazing new options that seek to help small communities develop sustainably and economically and new choices that allow visitors to better understand the culture and realities of the places they visit. A growing group of consumers want their travel to be less invasive, and emerging fair-trade tourism, anti-poverty tourism, and responsible tourism are changing the face of travel.

The term "responsible tourism" is a bit of a catch-all concept that includes an array of challenges and alternatives to mass tourism. For example, Responsibletourism.com covers efforts concerning fair-trade tourism, ecotourism, and protection of people who work in the travel industry. Responsible tourism is based on ethics and human rights-from protection of service workers and labor rights for mountain porters to programs against exploitation of women and children in tourism prostitution and campaigns against tourist trade in endangered species. It also means support for community-based travelers' programs-homestays, guest cottages, ethno-museums, and educational programs that bring tourist dollars directly into communities. Agro-tours, like fair trade coffee tours, are a good example.

Fair trade has been increasingly promoted by activists, farmers, business people, and even rockers like Coldplay's Chris Martin, who became a leading front man for fair trade after participating in an Oxfam trip to meet Haitian farmers. According to the group Fair Trade in Tourism South Africa (FTTSA), "Fair trade in tourism is about ensuring that the people whose land, natural resources, labor, knowledge, and culture are used for tourism activities actually benefit from tourism." In short, it means that tourism has an ethical framework and focuses on fair wages and long-term benefits for locals.

Tourism is not as easy to certify as coffee or textiles because it provides services (not just products) which are more difficult to monitor. There are some fledgling campaigns and projects underway. There are also many tour companies and organizations that link directly with fair-trade businesses and cooperatives and arrange tours to meet with and learn more about those efforts in countries like India, Thailand, Kenya, Cuba, and the Philippines.

Another emerging effort is the anti-poverty tourism movement. Closely linked with fair trade efforts, the anti-poverty campaign focuses on empowering local people to design their own sustainable communities, including tourism. The Eldis Gateway to Development Information is a resource web site hosted by several development agencies and includes pro-poor tourism case studies.

There are also anti-tourism efforts that are important for potential travelers to know about. Informed travelers can avoid supporting areas that are blatantly abusing human rights. There are numerous efforts around the globe working on all responsible tourism, and we are happy to report on some of these programs."

Grassroots Sustainable Tourism Organization

During my time in Bocas del Toro a couple months ago, I met Alexandra Dennis, the Bocas Sustainable Tourism

Alliance coordinator, and we spoke a bit about the BSTA's misson and the slow but steady movement toward low impact tourism in Central America. Because of my recent interest in sustainable tourism, I contacted Dennis a few weeks ago to discuss her organizations mission and challenges in more detail.

What is the BTSA's Mission?

"To support sustainable tourism development, promote responsible travel that sustain and enhance the geographical character of the place-our environment, culture, aesthetics, heritage, and the well-being of our residents while giving incentives for travelers to understand and protect the local culture and environment they are visiting."

How did the Idea for BTSA Come Around? Is this Part of an Umbrella Organization or Unique to Bocas?

Destination Management Organizations (DMOs) have proven to be effective at providing incentives for behavior change in the tourism sector. They also have the ability to strengthen links between tourism stakeholders and increase conservation awareness throughout the value chain. As such, through the generous support of the USAID-Conservation of Central American Watersheds program (CCAW), Solimar International was tasked with developing a DMO that can achieve the following objectives for the region:

- Enhance the competitiveness of sustainable tourism in Bocas del Toro;
- Support conservation efforts that mitigate environmental impacts;
- Respond to an increase in tourism demand; and
- Strengthen links between public and private sector groups within the destination.

As a result, the Bocas Sustainable Tourism Alliance (BSTA) was formed. BSTA is a local affiliate of Sustainable Travel International.

What are the requirements for an establishment to be accepted as an environmentally friendly property?

We are currently working through our guideline documents which include the details of acceptance. We require members to pledge to BSTA regarding their sustainable practices and work towards improving these practices on a regular basis. Our intention is to provide education on sustainable practices and to ensure that each of our members meets at least a certain threshold for sustainability.

What Exactly is Green Tourism? What can Establishments do to be More Green?

Sustainable tourism is tourism that is economically, culturally and environmentally sustainable. With sustainable tourism, cultural and environmental impacts are neither permanent nor irreversible. What is sustainable? Something that is capable of being maintained without exhausting available resources or causing damage. The aim of sustainable tourism is to ensure that tourism is a positive experience for local people, tourism companies and tourists themselves. Establishments can work towards improving their sustainability in a given area to that they meet the minimum standards and work towards being an example to other businesses.

What can Travelers do to Reduce their Carbon Footprint?

Here are some Green Travel Tips we provide for travelers on our website and on our Map of Bocas del Toro:

- Despite the huge amount of rainfall in this region, fresh water is in very short supply. Be aware of your usage when traveling - take short showers, re-use towels and linen at hotels, and team up with other travelers to wash a full laundry load.
- Trash is often dumped or burned, so recycle as much as you possibly can. BSTA's Tourist Information Center has containers for recycling plastic bottles, drink cans

and plastic bags, and Wongsa on the waterfront at the northern end of Calle 5 takes cleaned drinks cans and plastic bottles to Panama City for recycling.

- Don't keep buying plastic water bottles - refill your old one at the BSTA Tourist Information Center. It's cheaper, too!
- Do not touch coral or other sea life when diving or snorkeling. It could be harmful to you as well as to the coral! You can report any boat drivers who drop anchor on the coral or chase dolphins to BSTA, as well as any guides who act irresponsibly towards the environment.
- Do not purchase souvenirs made from coral or turtle shell, and avoid restaurants serving turtle meat or eggs. Lobsters are also overfished, so you may want to avoid ordering them too.
- Where possible, buy handicrafts directly from the communities or artisans to ensure your money reaches the craftspeople.. If you don't manage to visit a local community, a small selection of handicrafts are on sale at the BSTA Tourist Information Center, and all profits are returned to the craftspeople. Additionally, on the first and third Saturday of every month, local communities sell their own crafts, oils, coconut and cacao products at the Bocas Farmer's Market in the park.
- Give something back! Contact BSTA for information about volunteer opportunities in the region - from installing rainwater catchment systems to working in schools.
- Include a visit to a local community tourism project. You can stay in a cabin or with a family; enjoy a home-cooked meal; learn how medicinal plants are used; see how local crafts are made; and watch traditional dance performances.
- Look for low-impact tour options - hiking, biking, kayaking and snorkeling rather than motorized boats, cars or scooters.

THE ORGANIZATION FOR RESPONSIBLE TOURISM

International Attention through a Tourism Boycott. Stopping corruption at Belize borders is the key to stopping human traffickers from using Belize as a human trafficking superhighway. The Campaign to Stop Human Trafficking in Belize is supported by the Organization for Responsible Tourism. Organization for Responsible Tourism President Vivian Trill has appealed on behalf of the Campaign for Belize to tighten its borders. Thousands of human trafficking victims wind up in bars run by owners who profit form forced prostitution. The Campaign to Stop Human Trafficking in Belize is supported by the Organization for Responsible Tourism. Organization for Responsible Tourism President Vivian Trill has called for strengthening and enforcing liquor laws so they provide penalties to bar owners profiting from prostitution. The Campaign to Stop Human Trafficking in Belize has extended an invitation to work in partnership with Prime Minister Dean Barrow. The Campaign, through Organization for Responsible Tourism, has issued a number of Appeals to the Belize government urging immediate action to address human trafficking within and along its borders. Organization for Responsible Tourism President Vivian Trill has issued the Appeals on behalf of the Campaign.

- Fines for bar owners, starting at $2,000 (Belize) for a first offence
- Suspension of liquor license for a period of six months for the first offence, up to two years for the second, and up to five years for subsequent violations
- Monitor police enforcement of liquor license laws.

You can help us grow our on-line community that demands an end to sexual enslavement of girls in the Human Trafficking system of Central America. Five minutes of your time three times a week can make an immediate change. Using the power of the most democratic tool available today: Web, Email, Twit, blog and using your social networks to get the message out. The message? A community demanding a stop to sexual enslavement of girls in the human trafficking industries of Belize, Honduras and Guatemala.

In Kenya: Responsible Tourism Organization

Kenya is a country whose very name has long been synonymous with safari for seasoned and armchair travelers alike. An early leader in the preservation of game and its natural habitat, Kenya boasts more than 50 national parks and game reserves as well as private conservancies covering over 10 percent of its total landmass. The Big Five (lion, leopard, elephant, rhinoceros and buffalo) can all be found there, as well as cheetah, zebra, wildebeest, giraffe and many other carnivores and herbivores, large and small; and herds of minivans filled with awed tourists.

A large number of visitors is drawn to Kenya by visions of abundant game roaming across endless open spaces punctuated by the wide umbrellas of flat-topped acacias, and proud Masai in crimson robes herding their cattle in the distance. To accommodate these visitors, the country has developed one of Africa's most advanced tourism infrastructures, including large-scale accommodations, making it a favorite destination for group tourism. But as Kenya's popularity as a safari destination increased, so did the potential threat to its environment. Gamewatchers Safaris has been at the forefront of addressing the challenge of enhancing the tourism experience while giving landowners a chance to improve their quality of life in the present, and preserve land and wildlife for the next generations.

With its four Porini Camps (Amboselli Porini, Porini Rhino, Mara Porini and Porini Lion) Gamewatchers Safaris offered an innovative solution: small tented camps (between six and ten tents depending on the camp) on private conservancies located in close proximity to the famed Amboseli and Masai Mara National Parks; with the exception of Porini Rhino Camp, which was in the heart of one of the largest rhinoceros sanctuaries in East Africa, in the shadow of Mount Kenya. In these rigorously eco-friendly camps, great efforts were made to minimize the impact of the properties on the environment. No permanent structures were erected, power was exclusively solar generated, and all waste was managed according to strict procedures.

The host conservancies were on private land leased from the local Masai tribes who received financial benefits and employment opportunities as well as infrastructure development (such as roads and improved access to water). Local tribesmen had access to training in various aspects of the tourism industry and employment at the camps. As the time of my visit close to 90 percent of the camps' staff came from local tribes. Because of this close partnership, we, as camp guests enjoyed extensive contact with the local community, such nature walks with Masai Warriors, visits to the local villages where we were welcomed and allowed to observe the tasks of daily lives as well as celebration songs and dances. We were also able to enjoy nighttime game drives (these, like the walking safaris were not allowed in the National Parks). I especially enjoyed the opportunity for substantive conversations with my Masai guides about their tribes' history, current lives and aspirations.

Each camp was located in a spectacular site with its own game watching particularities. Click on the name of the camp to read about my memorable safari experience at each one of the Porini camps:

Amboselli Porini Camp was in the Selenkay Conservancy, adjacent to the north side of the Amboselli National Park, famous for the large herds of elephants roaming its sun-baked plains. Access to the park was via the conservancy's private road, against the eye-popping backdrop of Mount Kilimanjaro.

Porini Rhino Camp was located on the verdant plateau of the Ol Pejeta Conservancy, between the foothills of the Aberdares Range and the stately snow-capped peak of Mount Kenya. In addition to its large rhino population, it featured large herds of rarely seen herbivores such as reticulated giraffes and Grevy's zebras.

Mara Porini Camp was nestled in a soaring grove of yellow-barked acacia, within the Ol Kinyei Conservancy, ten miles away from the Northeast boundary of the Masai Mara National Reserve. The conservancy was host to a large resident pride of lions that I had the pleasure to observe repeatedly. Early morning game drives on my way to the park in the rolling meadows filled with herbivores browsing for their breakfast in the clear morning air were a special treat.

Porini Lion Camp was in the Olare Orok Conservancy on the northern border of the Masai Mara National Reserve. The abundance of "big cats" in the conservancy and this area of the park was such that it was hard to keep focused on any other game! Although the sight a pair of black rhinos engaged in courtship ritual did hold my attention, as did a breeding herd of elephants with several newborn calves; successfully tracking an elusive leopard was a high point of the visit, so was a pride of lions getting ready for their hunt. In the end the antics of a cheetah and her three tiny cubs won my cuteness award for the stay.

Another feature that further enhanced my game-watching experience was that all game drives took place in custom-built, open-sided Land Rovers, each with three tiers of two individual seats. Although the vehicles could accommodate up to six guests, there were never more than four of us in any vehicle, and more than once I had the pleasure of a private game drive. One slight drawback: it was sometimes a challenge to repress the urge to gloat a tiny bit as I met covetous glances coming from the air-conditioned minivans I occasionally passed in the parks.

N.B. Shortly after my visit, Porini Safari Camps and its parent company Gamewatchers Safaris were honored with the Responsible Tourism Award for "Best for Conservation of Endangered Species outside Protected Area" at the 2008 World Travel Market in London. The award, sponsored by Virgin Holidays, recognized Porini/Gamewatchers "for demonstrating that a high revenue, low impact tourism development approach can benefit the local Masai through developing conservancies and tourism in partnership with safari companies to create employment and community income and to conserve their land for wildlife."

Oman Hosts Forum

Around 500 participants from around the world took part at the fourth International Conference on Responsible Tourism in Destinations held in Oman this week.

Oman's Ministry of Tourism organised the event, from October 10 to 12 at the Intercontinental Hotel in Muscat, in collaboration with the UN World Tourism Organization (UNWTO) and the International Centre for Responsible Tourism, a post-graduate training and research centre in the UK's Leeds Metropolitan University.

Minister of Tourism Dr Rajiha Abdul Amir Ali hosted the conference together with Dr Harold Godwin from the centre who acted as co-chair.

The conference discussed topics previously unaddressed in responsible tourism conferences and presented real-world experiences. The participation of prominent international organizations such as UNWTO, the UN Environment Programme (UNEP), the UN Educational, Scientific and Cultural Organization (Unesco) and the International Union for Conservation of Nature (IUCN) provided a broad global perspective on the future of sustainable tourism.

The forum discussions focused on four interrelated themes: 'Tourism, Livelihoods, Local Economic Development and Human Resources;' 'Responsible Tourism in a World of Finite Resources;' 'The Responsible Tourist, Tangible and Intangible Heritage;' and 'Responsible Destinations and Marketing.'

"Oman's hosting of this prestigious international tourism event reflects the country's commitment to sustainable tourism development and its emphasis on the delivery of socio-economic benefits to local people while preserving and enhancing cultural and natural heritage. It provided a great opportunity for stakeholders including the government and private sectors as well as academic institutions and decision-makers to share ideas, discuss new developments and set new directions for principles and practices related to the development of responsible tourism," said Salem Al Mamari, director general of tourism promotions, Oman Ministry of Tourism.

Oman's main objectives for the forum were to contribute to the establishment of a general framework and relevant policies for responsible tourism in cooperation with international experts, to review and discuss the responsible tourism strategy of Oman, specifically its effective planning and management and its role in achieving economic development and the conservation of the Sultanate's environment and cultural heritage, and to enhance the international status of the Sultanate in general and the position of its tourism sector in particular.

The Travel Corporation Conservation Foundation

The Travel Corporation's (TTC) Conservation Foundation is the combined initiative of a number of leading travel companies. TTC is an enterprise owned by the Tollman family. Founded by Stanley Tollman more than fifty years ago, the company is headed today by his son Brett Tollman, who serves as CEO and President. The Travel Corporation's operations include leading niche travel brands such as Trafalgar Tours, the Red Carnations Hotels boutique collection, Uniworld's boutique river cruise ships and more.

With a sensitive awareness of environmental issues, TTC's Conservation Foundation is a non-profit organization dedicated to supporting sustainable tourism and protecting a few of the areas around the world that are culturally and ecologically threatened. Tollman's vision is to "continue to fund this important work" through the Travel Corporation's Conservation Foundation. Companies such as Trafalgar, Brendan Vacations, Insight Vacations, Uniworld Boutique River Cruise Collection, AAT Kings and others. Currently, the Conservation Foundation is entirely funded by its supporting travel companies. It has recently been involved in a number of projects in South America, Europe, Africa and Australia. The Foundation's Board of Directors carefully vets each and every project to ensure that funds are wisely and correctly used. The Board is supported with advice from an Advisory Panel of experts in the fields of conservation and development.

In South America, the Foundation contributed $350,000 towards the protection of the Atlantic Forest in Brazil, which has been designated a World Biosphere Reserve and contains many endangered species. Over the years the Forest has been widely cleared for sugar cane farming and urban settlement, and the remaining forest is estimated at less than 10% of the original area. The foundation grant helped protect some three million hectares of forest in high priority areas.

In Europe, Through the Foundation, Trafalgar is working with the UK's National Trust to protect a number of their areas, beginning with the Giant Causeway in Ireland this year (and the White Cliffs of Dover next year). Insight vacations is working to help protect and preserve some of the battlefields of Europe from the 1st and 2nd World Wars. Uniworld is working to clean up the River Nile and Contiki is working on an ocean initiative.

In Northern Botswana, Africa, the Foundation previously supported the Wilderness Wildlife Trust, which works towards supporting the African environment and wildlife. Specifically the funds have been earmarked for the construction and equipment of three research camps dedicated to the research of elephant, antelopes and zebra, to ensure the protection of both the species and their habitat.

In Australia, the beautiful Kimberly region has benefitted from Foundation funding over the past three years, which has gone towards helping local communities to develop and maintain sustainable tourism there. This will contribute both to protecting the environment and promoting an indigenous tourism industry, which in turn will support the local communities.

The World Travel and Tourism Council has held the Tourism for Tomorrow Awards for the last six years, and for the last three of these TTC's Conservation Foundation has been one of the two main co-sponsors, with Travelport. This award recognizes the leading organizations in the industry in promoting responsible tourism, an issue of major importance in a world of dwindling natural resources and ever-increasing concern for the environment.

TTC also believes that one of the most important impacts its collective efforts can contribute to reducing the carbon footprint of its travelers is to better educate the clients of its brands, to build their awareness and involvement in reducing their respective footprints during their journeys. This can be done by each of them always turning off their lights and air conditioning in the hotel rooms they stay in while away, and participating in the hotels' recycling and linen reuse programs when offered. Respecting local cultures and not polluting when visiting are also important. TTC works to engage and educate their clients before they travel on such matters to ensure the maximum awareness and take-up while they are travelling.

CHAPTER-9

ESTABLISHING THE COMMON GROUND

What does everyone already know about the issue? One of the best ways to attract the interest of an audience is to locate them on common ground, showing how the issue at hand has been or remains something about which they are already familiar and concerned. There are several ways to do this. Here are some examples:

- Present a New Angle
- Make an Emotional Appeal
- Present a Solution

Contract law holds that the positions of two parties prior to the existence of a negotiated contract, is one of zero interest for all participants. At some point two or more parties entering into a contract will find something of interest in the offerings that the other party has be it money in return for a set number of work hours a week, or, two items of a perceived value being traded. When parties overcoming zero interest positions begin to pursue interests, they need to bed down exactly what it is that will be discussed and what will not. This is commonly referred to as establishing common ground, shared interest or shaping and framing. Without establishing common ground, negotiations are difficult and unfocused. The likelihood of the parties invoking their BATNA's is very high.

Some writers on the subject note that the establishment of common ground is some of the most crucial time spent in any negotiation. Establishing common ground aids in the creation of focus in the exercise and similarly evokes a climate of certainty. To highlight this, one has but to cast one's mind to conditions of uncertainty. People generally experience anxiety and fear in these circumstances. It's clear enough.

Additional benefit accruing from the formulation of common ground is that it is far simpler to maintain focus on real issues. In the contrasting condition, one tends to concentrate on a plethora of issues which might help in translating the lay of the land - the one thing that has not been firmly bedded down. This may have adverse productivity implications and hence implications on the bottom line, whatever that may constitute.

Common ground is, however, not just for 'negotiators'. Given that forms of negotiation can be identified in many life situations and disciplines it stands to reason that the concept of common ground is, at least in theory, as pervasive. It would seem that in some form or other everybody seeks common ground. Terms often used in conjunction with common ground are framing and shaping. And it's not just 'negotiators' who frame, shape and seek common ground. One has but to look at project management, multidisciplinary academia and any number of other environments. Accept it, common ground is common. Mastering the art of common ground is of course more difficult.

Common ground is sought typically at the opening phases of a negotiation. Two or more parties will allocate time to flesh out what needs to be discussed, where it will be discussed and even where parties ought to be seated. Simply put, if you find yourself seeking answers to questions similar to "Why are we here", "What do we agree on", "What is keeping us apart", or, "When shall we deal with this" you are probably dealing with common ground in some form or other. Don't let the opportunity to shape its form slip away!

Common Ground in Other Disciplines

Project management theory espouses the creation of a shape and a frame of reference to particular pieces of work to be conducted. Ask any project manager about the biggest headaches in their field and invariably there can be only one response - 'scope creep'.

Scope creep is, as the name suggests, a shift or expansion of focus. It often occurs because work has not been described adequately or the customer feels that certain portions of work laid out within the plan are misaligned or do not address whatever new concerns have come to the fore. For any project to be managed effectively, tight reigns need to be kept on any changes, or the cart may soon careen off the path into the forest. The addition of even a single days' length to any activity noted on the Gantt chart can have significant cost and delivery implications.

Within academia there are a host of fields of knowledge, research and practice. Within each field there are more often than not a set of functions that concentrate exclusively on a number of particular specialisations. For instance within the field of Geography there are geomorphologists, climatologists, meteorologists, human settlement geographers, environmental geographers, cartographers, socialgeographers and the list grows everyday. Within each of these disciplines there may exist a number of prevailing views or theories that describe particular spatial and temporal interactions.

Quite intuitively academics in many fields have designed common ground for the areas of study under consideration. This is done through the creation of a language or a vocabulary pertaining to particular contract ideas that are distinct from one another e.g. alluvium - the sediments deposited through time by a riverine environment and colluvium - the sediment that slowly through time develops at the base of a hill or mountain having weathered from exposed formations in situ.

The terms refer to ideas or interactions that are known and for which consensus exists. From that consensual position the various parties can move forward to create a new language of consensus and solve and describe an ever greater ambit of interactions.

Most academics are familiar with numerous vocabularies, for example if a cartographer would be asked to create a map for a geomorphologist or a settlement geographer it is clear that her familiarity with both vocabularies would have to be consistent with her understanding of the vocabulary of her own field. Indeed the cartographer and the geomorphologist may well create a new vocabulary to suite their problems and solutions. In doing so they have created an 'opportunity of becoming' together. The purpose of the vocabulary is to keep the various parties involved on the same page or to create a common ground through which solutions are found and modelled.

To take this one step further one can imagine the challenge faced by academics and project managers involved in the Manhattan project, the project which had as its goal the creation of the atomic bomb. A host of skills in a large number of fields would have had to be aligned and kept on the same page for a period of time until the perceived fruits of that terrible project had been brought to bear.

The creation of common ground through terms of reference and vocabularies was absolutely vital. As important in that endeavour is the fact that none of the skill sets involved in that project had the wherewithal to pull it off successfully alone. The parties involved did not claim value but created it together according to a strictly managed and agreed upon set of principles - verbal contracts through interpersonal negotiation.

There are, as a matter of course, a large number of techniques which aid in the creation of shared aspirations and the management of difficult parties and interests towards basic framing and shaping. But perhaps more important than discussing the techniques, is the realisation of the spirit and the existence of the process within many, if not all fields of human endeavour, without which many human efforts would have come to nought.

Guiding Factors

The agent's role in handling a client is very important. Once a client enters the agency it becomes necessary for an agent to properly anticipate his needs and requirements. The client also has come with a predetermined notion about a destination he is visiting. WATA, the World Association of Travel Agencies, has prepared comprehensive guidelines for handling a client. These guidelines are based on the WATA Master-Key, an annual publication of the World Association of Travel Agencies. Updated and published yearly, the WATA Master-Key is a selectively comprehensive source of travel information. Individual agency tariffs given in the publication, represent the selling tool for members, incoming and outgoing services. Along with the tariffs the Master-Key gives a country description sheet containing a wealth of useful background information of a destination. In addition, the Master-Key also gives detailed information about some hotels located in important cities and tourist centres together with prevalent confidential tariffs and other relevant information for travel agencies.

The WATA Master-Key is a valuable reference material for travel agents. Its presentation makes it easy for the users to extract the information they need. The guidelines as enumerated in the Master-Key are as follows:

Sale of Tour : It should first be determined whether the client who wants to book a tour prefers to:

- Join an escorted tour, or
- Choose a FIT, combining leisure and activity according to his individual tastes and interests.

FIT/Your Relations with Client : If your client wants a "tailor made" tour, let him make the suggestions, without imposing your own views, on the following points:

Itinerary

- Determine the cities to be visited.
- Number of days (overnights) in each place.

- Mode of transportation between cities.
- Establish a rough time schedule, taking into consideration the time at his disposal.

Transportation

- Air transport should be used when time is limited and for long distances.
- Surface transportation should be recommended for shorter distances.
- For trains, determine whether advanced reservation is necessary. Indicate stations where trains are to be changed.
- Bus should be recommended in some countries, as it usually allows additional sightseeing.
- When arranging timetables, remember that your client is on vacation, and therefore avoid early departures.

Hotel Accommodation

Category of Hotels : Examine with your client which category of hotel he wants to stay at-Deluxe, First Class, Standard or Economy class. It is preferable that he is accommodated in a maximum rate room; however, if he must consider the cost, then rather suggest a lower grade hotel with best available room.

Type of Rooms : Examine whether your client wishes a special room on a special floor, with or without bath/ shower, sea view, outside or inside, etc. Draw his attention to the fact that in high season a room with a bath may be difficult to obtain in some places. In some cases a double room for single occupancy can be suggested, a single room being often small or not well situated. If your client insists on having a particular room, he may have to pay a supplement.

Meals : Ask your client whether he wants to have accommodation on bed and breakfast, demi-pension or full pension basis. If accommodation is on bed and breakfast basis, keep in mind that in certain resorts, demi or full pension is compulsory.

Check-in Time: Remind your client that check-in time at hotels is usually after 12 noon. Immediate occupancy on early morning arrivals can only be secured if the room is reserved for the previous night. If your client leaves late in the evening you may propose to him to pay for an additional night.

During periods of festivals, fairs or congresses, hotel space may not be available, rendering it necessary for your client to change the dates in those places; cabled hotel confirmation should, therefore, be suggested.

During periods, such as important festivals and events, a minimum stay of 5-7 days may be required. The same is applicable to some winter resorts, where a minimum stay of two weeks is required at Christmas and New Year.

Transfers

- The need of transfers upon arrival or departure results from the fact that it is often difficult to find one's way at airport, piers or stations with which one is not familiar.
- Transfers by agencies include interpreter meeting and assistance, accompanying clients (unless otherwise specified), porterage and transportation of 2 pieces of hand luggage per person between airport, station, bus or air terminal and hotels or vice versa, as well as tip to driver, but it does not include tip to hotel porter.
- Type of vehicle varies according to cities, generally by private car or taxi/cab.
- Airport transfers are naturally more expensive, but also the most convenient ones.
- When opting for transfer from city air terminal, your client must know that there will be no assistance at the airport, that he will have to tip for baggage at the airport

and pay for bus between the airport and the city terminal.

- Bus Arrivals: Certain bus companies stop at the major hotels to drop or collect clients, the disadvantage of this being the clients' dependence on time schedules and waiting for his turn to be dropped off. In addition, it will be necessary for the client to contact the local agency if other services are not to be provided in that city.

Sightseeing/Excursions/Tours

- The advantage of arranging sightseeing in advance is that your client does not have to waste his time, queuing up in the local agency. Also, a balance can be established in advance between leisure time and sightseeing, as well as for tours of the city and countryside.
- Motor Coach Tours : Apart from the economic viewpoint, there is the advantage of meeting other travellers, but clients have to arrange their own transportation to meeting points, as pick-up is very seldom done on motorcoach tours.
- Private Car Tours : Your client is picked up at the hotel, has the choice of time of departure and can stop wherever he likes, but this is the most expensive solution. In some places there are regular private car tours, or else sightseeing can be done on a seat-in-car basis.
- Hire of Private Car with Chauffeur
  - (a) City hire-must be recommended to deluxe clients, whose time is limited between trains, boats or planes, or who already know the city and want to see only special places or go shopping. Since very often the chauffeur cannot act as a guide, a private guide will be needed for sightseeing.

(b) Touring hire-if a private car is used for travelling from one city to another, local guides in each place will be sufficient. Distance covered daily should not exceed 250 km. Client's attention has to be drawn to the fact that he will have to pay for empty run of car (return to point of departure). The full daily basic charge is due, even if the vehicle is picked up in the evening.

- Motor Launch Tours/Boats Trips : The same applies here as for motor coach tours. Deluxe clients will be picked up at the hotel by private car and driven to embarkation pier.
- Self-driven cars can also be provided when clients fill the necessary conditions and, if wanted, a local guide can be placed at their disposal.

Music Festival, Theatre and Concert Tickets

Clients must be told that advance reservation is necessary. Confirmation of requested tickets cannot be guaranteed and tickets are not refundable unless they can be resold.

Land Arrangements : On the basis of all details furnished by your clients, it will enable you to make an estimate of the land arrangements.

Transatlantic/Pacific Transportation : To the land arrangements, the cost of flight/boat tickets for Transatlantic/ Pacific transportation has to be added.

Cost Price : Items a and b above give you the cost price.

Selling Price : In order to obtain the selling price you have to add your handling fees or mark-up, as well as a margin safeguarding any possible increase.

Suggested Itinerary

- A suggested itinerary should be drafted of what has been agreed with your client and submitted to him, together with the final price. The accompanying letter should clearly specify what is included in the price:

1. Price and type of land arrangements.
2. Price and class of air/sea/rail tickets, indicating that they are subject to change without notice.
3. The agency's conditions regarding handling charge, cancellation fees, possible deposit request, etc.

- It should also point out what is NOT included, such as cost of passport, visa, gratuities, tips to hotel porters, beverages, laundry, taxes (government, landing, embarkation), etc.
- Acceptance of suggested itinerary should be requested to enable you to proceed with reservation, and a deposit should be asked.

Your Relation with Service Suppliers : Reservation Procedures

- Once you are in possession of the client's agreement you can start reservations with carriers and hotels.
- In case your client requests only hotel reservations in a few places, it is advisable to make the reservations directly with the hotels.
- However, if transfer, sightseeing or other services are also requested, then it is preferable to go through the local agent, who is in a better position to replace a hotel by a similar one, in case of full occupancy.

Transfers : Due to frequent changes in time schedules and/ or due to changes your client may require, it is NOT advisable to send transfer requests earlier than one month prior to final documentation. An exception can be made if a special service is required and rate confirmation is needed.

Transfers should be requested by vouchers, indicating the following items:

- Full name of client(s) and number of passengers (for a child or an aged person give their age also).
- Date of transfer.

- Full description (indicate type of car, name of airport, city air terminal or station, exact flight or train number and arrival/ departure time).
- Name of hotel the client is staying at.
- Town and date of issue.
- If you do not have the rate of a service, request the rate of confirmation on the voucher copies.

Transportation : Whenever possible, obtain all tickets for rail, bus, boat, cruise, sleeping cars, etc., that may be required locally from agencies of foreign railroads, bus companies, steamship lines, etc.

Hotel Accommodation

- Depending on the time you have, hotel reservations can be made by reservation requests, by telex or cable (give paid reply), through hotel representatives, or through a WATA office. If you reserve through a a hotel representative or WATA office, their conditions should be respected.
- Once you have a hotel confirmation, issue a voucher for re- confirmation, indicating the following items:
  (a) Full name of client(s) and number of persons (for a child or an aged person give their age also).
  (b) Type of room.
  (c) Arrival and departure date, time of arrival and flight/ train number.
  (d) Meal conditions - clearly indicate whether rooms only, bed and breakfast (Continental or American/ English), half or full pension.
  (e) Always mention on hotel vouchers: "All taxes and service charges included".
  (f) Method of payment-indicate who will pay the bill. If the client settles the bill directly with the hotel, even when a deposit has been sent, hotels do not always pay a commission.

(g) Always ask for a re-confirmation of the rate on the voucher copies.

- If the best room is required, it should be determined as DELUXE, and a 10 per cent supplement foreseen.
- If a suite is required, it can be estimated a 2½ times the normal tariff.
- Whenever necessary, an extra night is to be foreseen for early arrival or late departure. Indicate on voucher early a.m. arrival the following day or request additional night or day use, advising the exact departure time.
- In case of split stays at the same hotel, a separate voucher should be issued for each day.

Sightseeing/Excursions/Tours

The same applies as for transfers - regular sightseeing tours should not be requested earlier than one month prior to the final documentation, except when a special service is required (e.g., sightseeing starting at airport) or for excursions/tours of two or more days' duration.

- Sightseeing/Excursions/Tours should be requested for WATA affiliates by vouchers, indicating the following items:

  (a) Full name of client(s) and number of persons (for a child or an aged person give their age also).

  (b) Date of sightseeing/excursions/tours.

  (c) Reference number of tour (if given), tour designation and title.

  (d) By private car or by regular scheduled motor coach.

  (e) For regular tours, give time and place of departure for private car tours, indicate "pick-up at hotel".

  (f) Name of hotel client is staying at.

  (g) Town and date of issue.

(h) In case a complete description does not appear in the agent's tariff, ask for additional information and rate confirmation.

- If your client wants to start a sightseeing tour from airport or station, add transfer-rate to sightseeing rate.

Chauffeur Driven Car Hire

- If private car hire with chauffeur is required, it has to be reserved in advance on the basis of rates quoted in the Master-Key. If rates are not given, apply to the agency for rates and details.
- For requests, issue voucher, indicating the following details:

  (a) Full name of client(s) and number of passengers.

  (b) Type of car (year of construction if available).

  (c) For city hire : Date and time of beginning of hire, length of hire or time of termination.

  (d) For touring hire: Date of beginning and termination of hire, starting time of hire and termination point, as well as stopovers.

  (e) Special requests, such as automatic cars, air conditioning, luggage, rack, etc.

  (f) Name of hotel client is staying at.

- City and Touring hire must be issued on separate vouchers, as tariffs and minimum daily averages are not the same. Also, if more than one day city hire is required issue one voucher for each day.
- Touring rate is established on the basis of a reliable map. Ten per cent of total mileage should be added for detours. If there are overnight stops, an additional 20 miles should be foreseen for possible use of car during the stay in city.
- For empty runs, it should be noted that the law does not authorise chauffeurs to drive more than 310 miles/

500 km per day, therefore, the total distance should be divided by this authorised maximum to reckon the number of chauffeur's overnights to be added to the touring rate.

- For chauffeur's accommodation, the rate appearing in the tariff has to be multiplied by the number of days the car has been used (special rates if outside the country).

Self-Driven Cars : If given, use rates appearing in the WATA Master-Key, otherwise, apply to the agency or consult Hertz, Avis, etc., for details and rates, whenever so indicated.

WATA Master-Key is a valuable document for a travel agent. The guidelines given in 'key' make the job of a travel agent a lot easier. As a comprehensive source of travel information it facilitates the work of a travel agent. The destination profiles provide a wealth of background information not only for a travel agent but also for a traveller. The 'key' is updated every year making it a valuable reference material.

IATA Accredition : Travel agents are the marketplace intermediaries responsible for selling the services of airlines worldwide. Considering the role and importance of air transport which is at the heart of travel and tourism selling, its services becomes the key motivation for engaging in travel agency business. Therefore, the importance of IATA approval for a travel agency is essential to enable it to sell the services of airlines.

For setting up a travel agency business there are no legal requirements. In some countries, however, governments exercise some kind of a licensing control over agencies. Most principals license the sale of their services through the issue of an agency contract, or agency agreement. In the absence of such a contract or an agreement, a travel agency will not get any commission from selling the services on behalf of the principal. The income of a travel agent is derived only from a commission which he receives from the principal after selling their services.

A licence is required by a travel agency for a commission to be payable on the sale of services of air carriers who are members of the International Air Transport Association. Domestic air services are, however, exempted from this. Most airlines want to sell their services worldwide but cannot do so on their own as it is not economically viable for them to set up extensive network of sales offices in every city of the world. It is the travel agents who are the marketplace intermediaries who make the sale of the services of the airlines possible worldwide through their own network.

As IATA travel makes up a substantial proportion of a total sale of a travel agency turnover, it is important for the travel agent who wishes to offer his clients the full range of travel services to obtain the necessary IATA approval or appointment.

IATA-Controlled Approval : The travel agency approval of IATA is controlled by its Agency Administration Board. This Board is made up of a number of IATA members operating from a particular country. Before approval is granted by IATA, a travel agency has to fulfil certain conditions. The most important condition is the demonstration by an agency of its financial soundness or financial standing. It has to prove that it has sufficient finances to settle the accounts of various airlines whose business it is handling. Another condition which an agency has to fulfil is to ensure the suitability and security of its premises. The premises of a travel agency are to be centrally located preferably in the centre of the town in a commercial district having proper security. The security aspect is very important as the agency has to keep the ticket stock of various airlines and this is quite expensive.

Proficiency of the staff of a travel agency is another important aspect which is considered by IATA before giving an approval. The staff has to be professionally trained in the handling of airlines business. IATA in association with UFTAA conducts the International Travel Agents Training Programme to meet the growing demand for a professionally trained manpower for the travel industry. The IATA-UFTAA training programme operates under the authority of the Passenger

Agency Training Board. IATA's Agency Training Services (ATS) located in Geneva (Switzerland) is responsible for the general administration of the programme.

In the field, the training programme is administered by a Local Coordinator who is responsible for the promotion of the training courses, the distribution of the training materials and the organisation of the examinations. The Local Coordinator is provided by the local IATA Agency Services, the National Airlines or the National Travel Agents Association in a particular country.

The IATA-UFTAA training courses have been designed primarily for travel professionals who work in IATA accredited travel agencies and whose main task is to sell international air transportation on behalf of IATA member airlines. The agents' staff can demonstrate proficiency by completing an IATA/UFTAA (passenger) training course.

The applicant's ability to generate new business is another requirement to be taken into consideration by IATA before considering an application for approval. This is to ensure that an agent is capable of generating new business in the market and has sufficient contacts to do so. To sum up, any travel agency, in order to get IATA approval for selling the services of IATA airlines worldwide, has to ensure the following:

- Financial standing
- Suitability of the premises
- Security for control of ticket stock
- Proficiency of the staff
- Ability to generate new business

After considering the above aspects and if the IATAs Agency Administration Board is satisfied, necessary IATA approval is accorded to an agency. Once approved, a Passenger Sales Agreement is issued and a numeric ticket validation code is provided which will be stamped on all tickets issued by that IATA-approved agent. IATA approval enables the agent to do business on behalf of all IATA members. It enables the agent to sell the services of all IATA member airlines throughout the world. The entire process of getting IATA approval can be quite time-consuming and lengthy and in the meantime agents applying for IATA approval are expected to generate business without getting any commissions.

Additional Approvals : In addition to the IATA approval which is basic for a travel agency, there are certain other approvals/recognitions required for running a travel agency. These approvals, however, will depend on the extent of activities and range of services which a particular agency would like to offer to its clients. For instance, in order to make commissionable sales on the services of railways, domestic airlines services and other principals such as car hire companies, shipping and cruise services, necessary approval is to be obtained. These approvals will enable travel agents to sell services on behalf of these principals with remuneration. In case a travel agency is an IATA-approved agent, or a member of the National Travel Agents Association, obtaining approvals for most of other principals becomes largely a formality.

Chapter-10

DEVELOPING COMMUNITY ENTERPRISE

Community development (CD) is a broad term applied to the practices and academic disciplines of civic leaders, activists, involved citizens and professionals to improve various aspects of local communities.

Community development seeks to empower individuals and groups of people by providing these groups with the skills they need to affect change in their own communities. These skills are often concentrated around building political power through the formation of large social groups working for a common agenda. Community developers must understand both how to work with individuals and how to affect communities' positions within the context of larger social institutions.

There are complementary definitions of community development. The Community Development Challenge report, which was produced by a working party comprising leading UK organisations in the field (including Community Development Foundation, Community Development Exchange and the Federation of Community Development Learning) defines community development as:

"A set of values and practices which plays a special role in overcoming poverty and disadvantage, knitting society together at the grass roots and deepening democracy. There is a CD profession, defined by national occupational standards and a body of theory and experience going back the best part of a century. There are active citizens who use CD techniques on a voluntary basis, and there are also other professions and agencies which use a CD approach or some aspects of it."

Community Development Exchange defines community development as:

"both an occupation (such as a community development worker in a local authority) and a way of working with communities. Its key purpose is to build communities based on justice, equality and mutual respect.

Community development involves changing the relationships between ordinary people and people in positions of power, so that everyone can take part in the issues that affect their lives. It starts from the principle that within any community there is a wealth of knowledge and experience which, if used in creative ways, can be channelled into collective action to achieve the communities' desired goals.

Community development practitioners work alongside people in communities to help build relationships with key people and organisations and to identify common concerns. They create opportunities for the community to learn new skills and, by enabling people to act together, community development practitioners help to foster social inclusion and equality.

A number of different approaches to community development can be recognized, including: community economic development (CED); community capacity building; Social capital formation; political participatory development; nonviolent direct action; ecologically sustainable development; asset-based community development; faith-based community development; community practice social work; community-based participatory research (CBPR); Community Mobilization; community empowerment; community participation; participatory planning including community-based planning (CBP); community-driven development (CDD); and approaches to funding communities directly.

Education and the community-wide empowerment that increased educational opportunity creates, form a crucial component of community development and certainly for underserved communities that have limited general educational and professional training resources. Workforce development and the issues and challenges of crossing the Digital divide, and increasing community-wide levels of Digital inclusion have become crucially important in this and both for affordable access to computers and the Internet, and for training in how to use and maintain these resources.

Local communities that cannot connect and participate in the larger and increasingly global Online community are becoming increasingly marginalized because of that. So where Urban development with its focus on buildings and physical infrastructure was once viewed as a primary path forward to community development, development of computer and online infrastructure and access, and the community enablement they support have to become central areas of focus moving forward. This has become an area of active involvement for both public and private sector organizations including foundations and nonprofit organizations. In the United States, nonprofit organizations such as Per scholas seek to "break the cycle of poverty by providing education, technology and economic opportunities to individuals, families and communities" as a path to development for the communities they serve.

Community development has been a sometimes explicit, sometimes implicit goal of community people, aiming to achieve, through collective effort, a better life, and has occurred throughout history.

In the 19th century, the work of the early socialist thinker Robert Owen (1771-1851), sought to create a more perfect community. At New Lanark and at later communities such as Oneida in the USA and the New Australia Movement in Australia, groups of people came together to create utopian or intentional utopian communities, with mixed success.

In the United States in the 1960s, the term "community development" began to complement and generally replace the idea of urban renewal, which typically focused on physical development projects often at the expense of working-class communities. In the late 1960s, philanthropies such as the Ford Foundation and government officials such as Senator Robert F. Kennedy took an interest in local nonprofit organizations-a pioneer was the Bedford-Stuyvesant Restoration Corporation in Brooklyn-that attempted to apply business and management skills to the social mission of uplifting low-income residents and their neighborhoods. Eventually such groups became known as "Community Development Corporations" or CDCs. Federal laws beginning with the 1974 Housing and Community Development Act provided a way for state and municipal governments to channel funds to CDCs and other nonprofit organizations. National organizations such as the Neighborhood Reinvestment Corporation (founded in 1978 and now known as NeighborWorks America), the Local Initiatives Support Corporation (founded in 1980 and known as LISC), and the Enterprise Foundation (founded in 1981) have built extensive networks of affiliated local nonprofit organizations to which they help provide financing for countless physical and social development programs in urban and rural communities. The CDCs and similar organizations have been credited with starting the process that stabilized and revived seemingly hopeless inner city areas such as the South Bronx in New York City.

Community planning techniques drawing on the history of utopian movements became important in the 1920s and 1930s in East Africa, where Community Development proposals were seen as a way of helping local people improve their own lives with indirect assistance from colonial authorities.

Mohondas K. Gandhi adopted African community development ideals as a basis of his South African Ashram, and then introduced it as a part of the Indian Swaraj movement, aiming at establishing economic interdependence at village level throughout India. With Indian independence, despite the continuing work of Vinoba Bhave in encouraging grassroots land reform, India under its first Prime Minister Jawaharlal Nehru adopted a mixed-economy approach, mixing elements of socialism and capitalism.During the fifties and sixties, India ran a massive community development programme with focus on rural development activities through government support. This was later expanded in scope and was called integrated rural development scheme [IRDP]. A large number of initiatives that can come under the community development umbrella have come up in recent years.

Community Development became a part of the Ujamaa Villages established in Tanzania by Julius Nyerere, where it had some success in assisting with the delivery of education services throughout rural areas, but has elsewhere met with mixed success. In the 1970s and 1980s, Community Development became a part of "Integrated Rural Development", a strategy promoted by United Nations Agencies and the World Bank. Central to these policies of community development were:

- Adult Literacy Programs, drawing on the work of Brazilian educator Paulo Freire and the "Each One Teach One" adult literacy teaching method conceived by Frank Laubach.
- Youth and Women's Groups, following the work of the Serowe Brigades of Botswana, of Patrick van Rensburg.
- Development of Community Business Ventures and particularly cooperatives, in part drawn on the examples of José María Arizmendiarrieta and the Mondragon Cooperatives of the Basque Region of Spain
- Compensatory Education for those missing out in the formal education system, drawing on the work of Open Education as pioneered by Michael Young.
- Dissemination of Alternative Technologies, based upon the work of E. F. Schumacher as advocated in his book Small is Beautiful: Economics as if people really mattered
- Village Nutrition Programs and Permaculture Projects, based upon the work of Australians Bill Mollison and David Holmgren.

- Village Village Water Supply Programs

Community development in Canada has roots in the development of co-operatives, credit unions and caisses populaires. The Antigonish Movement which started in the 1920s in Nova Scotia, through the work of Doctor Moses Coady and Father James Tompkins, has been particularly influential in the subsequent expansion of community economic development work across Canada.

In the 1990s, following critiques of the mixed success of "top down" government programs, and drawing on the work of Robert Putnam, in the rediscovery of Social Capital, community development internationally became concerned with social capital formation. In particular the outstanding success of the work of Muhammad Yunus in Bangladesh with the Grameen Bank, has led to the attempts to spread microenterprise credit schemes around the world. This work was honoured by the 2006 Nobel Peace Prize.

The "Human Scale Development" work of Right Livelihood Award winning Chilean economist Manfred Max Neef promotes the idea of development based upon fundamental human needs, which are considered to be limited, universal and invariant to all human beings (being a part of our human condition). He considers that poverty results from the failure to satisfy a particular human need, it is not just an absence of money. Whilst human needs are limited, Max Neef shows that the ways of satisfying human needs is potentially unlimited. Satisfiers also have different characteristics: they can be violators or destroyers, pseudosatisfiers, inhibiting satisfiers, singular satisfiers, or synergic satisfiers. Max-Neef shows that certain satisfiers, promoted as satisfying a particular need, in fact inhibit or destroy the possibility of satisfying other needs: eg, the arms race, while ostensibly satisfying the need for protection, in fact then destroys subsistence, participation, affection and freedom; formal democracy, which is supposed to meet the need for participation often disempowers and alienates; commercial television, while used to satisfy the need for recreation, interferes with understanding, creativity and identity. Synergic satisfiers, on the other hand, not only satisfy one particular need, but also lead to satisfaction in other areas: some examples are breast-feeding; self-managed production; popular education; democratic community organizations; preventative medicine; meditation; educational games. 'Bold text'

Rural community development encompasses a range of approaches and activities that aim to improve the welfare and livelihoods of people living in rural areas. As a branch of community development, these approaches pay attention to social issues particularly community organizing. This is in contrast to other forms of rural development that focus on public works (e.g. rural roads and electrification) and technology (e.g. tools and techniques for improving agricultural production).

Rural community development is important in developing countries where a large part of the population is engaged in farming. Consequently, a range of community development methods have been created and used by organisations involved in international development. Most of these efforts to promote rural community development are led by 'experts' from outside the community such as government officials, staff of Non-governmental organizations and foreign advisers. This has led to a long debate about the issue of participation, in which questions have been raised about the sustainability of these efforts and the extent to which rural people are - or are not - being empowered to make decisions for themselves.

In the UK rural community development is seen as very important. Rural areas are often some of the most deprived in the country. Rural Community Councils around the country support local rural communities in securing sustainable futures. The local rural communities are supported by experienced community development workers.

In the United States, rural community development is an essential tool in keeping rural areas economically viable in a competitive global arena. Under the United States Department of Agriculture, this is addressed through the Rural

Development mission area, comprising the Rural Housing Service, Rural Utilities Service, and Rural Business-Cooperative Service. Research and data sources for rural areas of the United States is also addressed by the United States Department of Agriculture through the Economic Research Service and the National Agricultural Library's Rural Information Center.

Part of the United States Department of Commerce, the Economic Development Administration (EDA) is tasked within it's mission "to generate jobs, help retain existing jobs, and stimulate industrial and commercial growth in economically distressed areas of the United States. EDA assistance is available to rural and urban areas of the Nation experiencing high unemployment, low income, or other severe economic distress."

There are four Regional Rural Development Centers in the United States that coordinate "rural development research and extension (education) programs cooperatively with the land-grant institutions regionally and nationally. The Centers support and strengthen individual state efforts in rural areas by developing networks of university research and extension faculty from a variety of disciplines to address rural issues."

Urban Renewal

Urban renewal is a program of land redevelopment in areas of moderate to high density urban land use. Renewal has had both successes and failures. Its modern incarnation began in the late 19th century in developed nations and experienced an intense phase in the late 1940s - under the rubric of reconstruction. The process has had a major impact on many urban landscapes, and has played an important role in the history and demographics of cities around the world.

Urban renewal may involve relocation of businesses, the demolition of historic structures, the relocation of people, and the use of eminent domain (government purchase of property for public use) as a legal instrument to take private property for city-initiated development projects.

In some cases, renewal may result in urban sprawl and less congestion when areas of cities receive freeways and expressways.

Urban renewal has been seen by proponents as an economic engine and a reform mechanism, and by critics as a mechanism for control. It may enhance existing communities, and in some cases result in the demolition of neighborhoods.

Many cities link the revitalization of the central business district and gentrification of residential neighborhoods to earlier urban renewal programs. Over time, urban renewal evolved into a policy based less on destruction and more on renovation and investment, and today is an integral part of many local governments, often combined with small and big business incentives.

Trust for Developing Communities (TDC)

The Trust delivers community development work across Brighton & Hove and Sussex, devises work-led training schemes in community development and provides consultancy and research services. Our work with local community groups supports them to develop and flourish and represent their own neighbourhoods in local governance bodies and city wide strategic partnerships. The Trust is committed to provide the highest standard of consultancy and community development training, through:

- Its accredited Working in Community Organisations (WICO) course
- Specially designed courses to suit the needs of different client groups
- Specific consultancy projects, including monitoring and evaluation

Developing Communities Project, Inc. (DCP)

Developing Communities Project, Inc. (DCP) works through congregations, neighborhood groups, and organizations to engage, train, and empower grassroots leaders to organize the residents of Greater Roseland to advocate for services and public policies that improve their quality of life. When adverse and inequitable conditions are ameliorated, families are strengthened and the community is collectively redeemed.

The Mortenson Center in Engineering for Developing Communities (MC-EDC)

The Mortenson Center in Engineering for Developing Communities (MC-EDC) promotes integrated and participatory solutions to humanitarian development by educating globally responsible engineering students and professionals to address the problems faced by developing communities worldwide.

Engineering for Developing Communities (EDC) is one of several Active Learning Opportunities and Exploration Beyond the Classroom experiences available to students in the College of Engineering and Applied Science at the University of Colorado at Boulder.

The Mortenson Center in Engineering for Developing Communities (MC-EDC) presents a unique opportunity for educating a new generation of GLOBAL engineers who contribute to the relief of the problems faced by developing communities worldwide. The center emphasizes an integrated and participatory nature of humanitarian development. As such, it contributes to meeting the UN Millennium Development Goals. MC-EDC encompasses education, research & development, and outreach/service related to sustainable community development. All MC-EDC students are assigned to real projects.

MC-EDC offers a EDC Graduate Certificate in the MS/PhD programs in Environmental Engineering, Civil Systems, Construction Engineering and Management, and Building Systems. Limited MC-EDC research assistantships are available for graduate students, typically starting in the fall semester. In addition, Mortenson Center Graduate Fellowships are awarded in the spring.

EDC graduate students are eligible for participation in the Western Regional Graduate Program. EDC can offer in-state tuition rates to graduate students with legal residency in any of the 14 Western states in WRGP. For more information, please contact Robyn Sandekian.

Undergraduate students should consider enrolling in the International Engineering Certificate in French, Spanish or Chinese. The IEC provides students with a solid base of language and culture coursework that can prepare students to engage in work with developing communities.

MC-EDC serves as a blueprint for the education of engineers of the 21st century who are called to play a critical role in contributing to peace and security in an increasingly challenged world.

Community Enterprise Centre

The Community Enterprise Centre has now been open since October 2007 and provides a flexible and affordable base for several voluntary and community groups. The Community Enterprise Centre offers groups many advantages including access to a community development worker who is able to help with funding and help steer organisations towards sustainability.

Another advantage for organisations using the Community Enterprise Centre is that the centre has quickly become a social space; this gives groups the opportunity to work in partnership and network freely with other voluntary and community organisations.

The Community Enterprise Centre's facilities enables established groups to hire permanent office space, but the CEC also offers the flexibility of shared office space including computer and internet for fledgling groups. In addition both established and fledgling organisations can hire event space at a very realistic rate.

Organisations and projects currently residing at the centre are:

- Bora Shabba
- CRUSE Bereavement Care
- DOC All Change Project
- DOC (Developing Our Communities)
- Gvants
- Hidden Voices
- Hull Gypsy Traveller Project
- Humber All Nations Alliance (H.A.N.A)
- Russian Communities of Hull
- T.E.F.A

The event space is also available for hire by the private and public sector and this aspect of the Community Enterprise Centre's work is crucial to its success. It is through attracting the public and private sector to use our facilities that the CEC will be able to achieve sustainability and ensure that we can continue to offer low rents to the third sector.

If you feel that your organisation could benefit from the Community Enterprise Centre's facilities please don't hesitate to contact the CEC staff who will be able to arrange a time for you to visit the centre and discuss ways that we can work together in partnership.

Community of Practice (CoP)

A lot of learning is social, which means it occurs in some type of group setting. The basic premiss developed by Lave and Wenger is that CoPs are everywhere and at we are involved in a number of them at work, school, and home. In some CoP groups we might be core members, while in others, we are more at the margins. These social groups increase our chances of learning. Jean Lave and Etienne Wenger (1991) described a Community of Practice as "a set of relations among persons, activity and world, over time and in relation with other tangential and overlapping CoPs".

A CoP defines itself along three dimensions:

- What it is about: A joint enterprise understood and continually renegotiated by its members.
- How it functions: A mutual engagement that bind members together into a social entity.
- What capability it has produced: The shared repertoire of communal resources (routines, sensibilities, artifacts, vocabulary, styles, etc.) that members have developed over time.

These community of practices normally go through five stages:

- **Potential**: People face similar situations without the benefit of a group to help.
- **Coalescing**: People come together and recognize the potential of forming a group.
- **Active**: The members of a group develop a community of practice.
- **Dispersed**: Members no longer engage very intensely, but the community still lives as a center of knowledge for the group. The community is no longer central, but people still remember it as a significant part of their lives.

A CoP involves organizing around some particular area of knowledge that gives members a sense of joint enterprise and identity. It also involves developing a set of relationships over time and developing communities around things that matter to its members. For a CoP to function, it needs to generate a shared repertoire of ideas, commitments and memories. In addition, it also needs to develop resources, such as tools, documents, routines, vocabulary and symbols that carry the wealth of knowledge within the community.

Travel and Trade Associations

Formation of associations by independent firms in a particular trade or a group of industries is primarily done with a view to protecting the interests of its members. Trade

Organisations are voluntary bodies formed by individual firms belonging to a particular trade not only to protect but also to advance the common interests of their members. The main objective of forming an association by independent firms is to get strong representations which act as channels of communication with the government and other organised groups to further the interests of their members. In almost all disciplines, members sharing similar interests or complementing each other's interests in some way or other have formed organisations/associations.

The ever-increasing importance of the tourism sector and the increase in the growth in its volume over the years have resulted in the formation of associations in this sector. Secondly, the ever-increasing international character of the modern day tourism and the growing influence of international agencies in various fields have also influenced the growth of international cooperations in the field of tourism. All these developments in turn have brought together members of the travel associations at national, regional and international levels collectively to further their trade interests. Different producers and sellers of various tourist services like tour operators, travel agents, hotel companies, airline companies, ground operators, etc., have formed associations of their members.

The scope of discussion in this chapter is limited to the associations of travel agents and tour operators. These associations today have assumed great importance and provide a platform to their members where ideas are exchanged and topics of mutual interest discussed and solutions arrived at. They provide services like information, assistance and advice in the conduct of their business to their members. The various associations in the field of tourism can take different forms. Broadly, the following five forms can be identified:

- Those based on the education and training needs of the industry. These may include professional bodies like Hotel and Catering Management Association, Travel and Tourism Management Association which are primarily concerned with the training and educational standards of personnel working in hotel and travel agencies.

- Those which are concerned with the sectoral interests of their members. They include the National Associations of Travel Agents and Tour Operators. Each country has such associations. For instance, the American Society of Travel Agents (ASTA), the Australian Federation of Travel Agents (AFTA), the Association of British Travel Agents (ABTA), the Japan Association of Travel Agents (JATA), the Indian Association of Travel Agents (IATA), the Swiss Travel Agents Association, the German Travel Agencies' Association, etc.
- Those which are responsible for developing, promoting and facilitating tourism among a particular region. These regional organisations draw their membership from public or private sector organisations dealing with tourism and sharing a common interest in the promotion and development or marketing of a specific tourism geographical area or a region. This area may represent a region, a state, a country or a resort. The membership is opened to groups or organisations, both in public and private sectors, rather than individuals, such as Pacific Area Travel Association (PATA), etc.
- Those which are concerned with the promotion and development of tourism globally. These organisations deal with all the aspects of tourism. The rapid expansion in tourism activity globally was responsible for creating a need for world bodies to deal with tourism issues at the government level. The World Tourism Organisation (WTO) is one such global tourism organisation representing public sector tourism from most countries of the world.
- Those which are responsible for promoting and furthering interests of specific trade groups in the travel industry, like travel agents, and tour operators at the global level. Unlike the sectoral trade association of

travel agents and tour operators, these have international impact. They play an important role in representing the common interests of travel agents and tour operators worldwide in crucial international issues like negotiation of travel agency commission rates with International Air Transport Association (IATA). Universal Federation of Travel Agents Association (UFTAA) and the World Association of Travel Agencies (WATA) are such associations. Both UFTAA and WATA play an important role in representing the interests of travel agents worldwide. The following pages will discuss in detail the roles and functions of these two international organisations of travel agents.

Universal Federation of Travel Agents Association (UFTAA) : Universal Federation of Travel Agents Association (UFTAA), an important organisation of travel agents on a worldwide basis, was founded in Rome in November, 1966 by the merger of the International Federation of Travel Agencies (IFTA) and the Universal Organisation of Travel Agents' Associations (UOTAA). The General Secretariat of UFTAA is located in Monaco.

The membership of the Federation consists of the National, Travel Agents' Associations from most of the countries in the world. Today it represents over 33,000 travel agencies globally. National Travel Agents Associations are the full members of UFTAA. The membership of the Federation is split into nine regions each covering a group of countries.

The Aims of the Federation : The following are the main aims of the federation :

- To act as the negotiating body with the various branches of tourism and travel industry on behalf of its members and also in the interest of the public;
- To ensure for all travel agents through their national associations the maximum degree of cohesion and understanding, prestige and public recognition, advancement of the member's interest and protection from legislation and legal points of view; and

- To offer to its member all the necessary professional and technical advice and assistance in matters concerning their trade.

UFTAA provides several advantages to its members which include the right to reproduce the symbol on the stationery, information service on all matters of legal or professional nature, free of charge assistance by its Legal Department for the recovery of outstanding debts, arbitration services for litigations between a member agency and a hotel company in different countries, etc.

The Annual General Assembly of UFTAA is the policymaking body. The Assembly decides on the general policy of the Federation and makes recommendations on any matter within its competence. The Board of Directors, consisting of Directors elected from candidates proposed by National Member Associations handle the routine business of the Federation. The Executive Committee is responsible for handling day-to-day activities and also urgent matters. The UFTAA world congress which normally takes place annually is the advisory body of the Federation. The world congress is open to UFTAA registered agents and enterprises, UFTAA individual members, suppliers of services and regional, national and international public authorities.

UFTAA claims to have a series of achievements since its inception in the year 1966. Prominent among its achievements is its collaboration with the International Rail Union resulting in obtaining increased commission on several railway networks, creation of professional training courses and introduction of Rail inclusive Tours. With regard to air transport, the cooperation between the Federation and IATA over a number of years has resulted in the raising of commission, introduction of an overriding commission, 50 per cent reduction for the spouses of travel agents and creation of international correspondence courses for the training of agency sales staff. In the sphere of hotel industry, the federation, following negotiations with the International Hotel Association has created an international convention, setting down regulations for booking, and cancellation fees. A court of arbitration to settle disputes between hotels and travel agents located in different countries has also been created.

World Association of Travel Agencies (WATA)

WATA, the World Association of Travel Agencies, is another important worldwide association representing travel agencies. Founded in the year 1949, WATA is a non-profit organisation created by independent travel agents for the benefit of all travel agencies around the world. The Association has over 200 members from 175 cities in 80 countries. The headquarters of WATA are located in Geneva, Switzerland.

The basic idea of WATA is to bring together local travel agencies into an international network, so that every member is offered all the facilities and advantages of being associated with an international body in addition to enjoying local prominence. WATA is registered as an association under Swiss Civil Law, and is essentially a non-profit making organisation. Under its statutes, WATA and its members are required to assist one another.

The General Assembly of WATA held every year provides a forum for discussion of the Association's business and an opportunity to talk with fellow members. It enables members to have an exposure to new business and ideas applied successfully elsewhere. One day, before the General Assembly, the meetings of the Regional Assemblies are held which provide a chance to its members to discuss regional travel problems as well as the implementation on the regional level of the decisions taken by WATA governing bodies. The regions also have the possibility to submit to the General Assembly ideas and suggestions.

Advantages of a WATA Membership : The advantages of WATA membership include:

Guaranteed Payment of IHA Invoices : WATA headquarters guarantees payment of all invoices for services rendered by the International Hotel Association (IHA) hotel members to WATA members, up to a certain amount. In return, the IHA has requested its members to accept vouchers for individual clients issued by WATA members to be billed after the client's departure.

Internal Guarantee : Subject to certain conditions, unsettled services rendered by one WATA member agency to another, are paid by WATA headquarters.

WATA Standard Exchange Voucher : An agency's own exchange voucher bearing the WATA logo and the reference to the IHA/WATA agreement or the standard WATA exchange voucher printed by the headquarters with the name of agency, are widely accepted by hotels worldwide. In the majority of the cases, hotels accepting these vouchers will agree to bill the services after the departure of the clients without prepayment or deposit.

Membership List and Introduction Card : A small booklet listing all WATA members and their addresses is available for agencies to give to clients who go on extended trips, in case they need assistance and service en route. For specially important clients, a special introduction card is available for the members.

WATA Master-Key : Updated and published yearly, the WATA Master-Key is a comprehensive source of travel information. Individual WATA agency tariffs represent an invaluable selling tool for members' incoming and outgoing services. Master-Key carries the tariffs of WATA members offering incoming services. A standard presentation makes it easy for users to extract the information they need. Along with the tariffs is a country description sheet provided by the respective National Tourist Offices containing a wealth of background information.

WATA Circular Letters for Latest Developments : This internal newsletter keeps members abreast of new developments in WATA. It also gives members an opportunity to describe special activities of their own.

WATA's Overriding Commission : A supplementary commission of 5 per cent is allowed between members, on prices published in WATA Master-Key for transfers, sightseeing, excursions, tours and chauffeur-driven car hire.

WATA Membership Categories

Full Members : Membership in WATA is open to any travel agency, preferably privately-owned, which can prove a sound financial structure, adheres to the highest professional ethics expected in the industry and enjoys prominent standing in the local community.

All WATA members have the same rights, privileges and obligations within the association. Individual members are grouped into three sub-categories depending on the scope of their activities, as follows:

- Agencies offering both outgoing and incoming services.
- Agencies offering outgoing activities only.
- Agencies offering incoming service only.

Associate Members : A travel agency may apply to become an associate member. This category offers the possibility to become a WATA associate member for a trial period of 2 years. The associate members have the same rights and obligations as the full members but the fees are generally reduced.

Allied Members : A category open to hotels, airlines, shipping lines and car hire companies. The aim of this category is to develop the business relations between the members and their partners. Allied members may attend the WATA General Assembly, they will be listed in the WATA publications, receive all WATA publications and circulate letters and have the right to display on all their printed matter, the WATA logo created for this category. They have no voting right nor can they be elected to the WATA governing bodies. Both UFTAA and WATA are playing a valuable role in representing the interests of travel agents worldwide. In addition to the above two international travel associations representing travel agents, there are some important national travel agents organisations like the American Society of Travel Agents (ASTA) which has influence beyond the confines of USA. The American Society of Travel Agents draws its membership not only from travel agents and principals within the country but also from principals throughout the world who have interest in promoting overseas tourism from United States to their country.

THE AMERICAN SOCIETY OF TRAVEL AGENTS (ASTA)

American Society of Travel Agents (ASTA) is the leading professional society of travel agents in the USA. The world's largest professional travel trade association, ASTA was established in New York in the year 1931. Originally named the American Steamship and Tourist Agent's Association, the present name was adopted in the year 1944. The Society was established to foster programmes for the advancement of the travel agency industry, promote ethical practices and provide a public forum for travel agents. It has now over 25,000 members and is the only organisation representing all segments of the travel industry. The membership consists of travel agents, carriers, hotels, etc.

Purpose : The purpose of ASTA is the promotion and advancement of the interests of the travel agency industry and the safeguarding of the travelling public against fraud, misrepresentation and other unethical practices. The Society maintains legal representation and also a Government Affairs office in Washington, D.C. to provide direct contact with the Federal Government and the regulatory agencies in the travel and transportation field, and to protect the legitimate interests of travel agents.

Services : ASTA's services to travel agents also benefit the general public. Such activities include sponsorship of frequent conferences on travel matters, involving airlines, steamship companies, agents, municipal and government officials, and other interested parties; discussions with airlines on fare structures and travel destinations; research studies into traveller preferences; close cooperation with various city, state and government agencies across the country in travel-oriented matters, assistance to all agencies across the country in travel-oriented matters; assistance to all levels of government consumerism departments in upgrading standards of service to travellers.

The American Society of Travel Agents is primarily the trade association of the travel agency industry. There are more than 25,000 members in the Society covering all segments of the travel industry. Out of the total membership of 25,000 over 14,000 are travel agents in the United States of America and Canada. In addition to travel agents, there are allied members representing airlines, railways, hotels, government tourist offices, etc. The Society has a membership in over 140 countries all over the world. In order to qualify for the membership of the Society, an applicant must be in the business of travel under its present ownership or control for a minimum period of three years.

Membership : There are two basic classifications of membership-Active and Allied. Active members are year-round travel agents or tour operators. Allied members include airlines and steamship companies, railroad, bus lines, car rental firms, hotels, resorts, government tourist offices and other organisations regularly engaged in the travel industry or associated industries.

ASTA has over 2,500 travel agency members outside the USA and Canada. All are engaged in travel agency operations on a year-round basis and have been in business for at least three consecutive years. The international roster has its own elected governors and actively participates in all phases of Society meetings. International members come from Algeria, Bolivia, Sri Lanka, Denmark, Ethiopia, Fiji Island, Ghana, India, Iran, Japan, the Netherlands, Portugal, South Africa and Sweden.

ASTA World Travel Congress : The year's foremost meeting place is the ASTA World Travel Congress. The Congress is the single most important meeting held annually in the travel industry and the programme includes workshops, seminars, business meetings, film presentations, and social events. Members from throughout the world travel industry participate, give talks, lead discussion groups and conduct sessions. The ASTA World Travel Congress has been the platform for launching many important and beneficial education programmes for agents. The Congress grants Travel Hall of Fame awards, an honour given to those whose careers have made long standing impacts on the development and expansion of the travel industry and tourism. The awards are given every year to outstanding members. ASTA consists of the following departments:

- Policy implementation
- Administration
- Industry relations
- Membership relations
- Communication

The members of the society derive various advantages which include education and training. ASTA has a comprehensivc list of travel courses and seminars which are attended by its members. The society also offers professional training courses to senior travel agency personnel. Various research papers and newsletters are brought out from the Society's headquarters for use of its members.

ASTA Chapters : The society has 28 chapters in the United States of America and Canada and another 28 chapters overseas. Each chapter has elected officers and appointed committees. There is a National Board of Directors which establishes policies of the Society. Every two years a new President and Chairman of the Board are elected by Active Members. Day-to-day activities of the Society are looked after by a professional staff which works under the guidance of an Executive Vice-President who, in fact, is the Chief Operating Officer of the society and makes recommendations on policy matters to the Board and Executive Board. The Vice-President directs the headquarters staff in providing a broad programme of services and facilities to ASTA's membership and carrying on the day-to-day business of the Society. ASTA world headquarters are located in New York City, USA.

CHAPTER-11

FAIR TRADE IN TOURISM MARKETING TOOL

The Hostel has been Accredited by Fair Trade in Tourism (a trade mark awarded to businesses that adhere to fair trade criteria, fair wages and working conditions, fair operations, purchasing and distribution of benefits, ethical business practices and respect for human rights, culture and the environment). Through empowering them with life changing skills they become stakeholders, to share in the profits and to actively play a wider role in the running and accountability of our business.

By being a member of Fairtrade, we acitively promote the ideals and principles of this organisation. These principals are:

- Fairshare
- Democracy
- Respect
- Reliability
- Transparency
- Sustanibality

In 2007 we hired a company called Clear Insight, which is run by Val Toledo, who introduced a value system together with our staff. The 8 values which all of us adhere to are:

- Trust, Honest,Integrity, Respect, Service, Health, Responsibility, Upliftment and Recognition.

Through various workshops and in a fun way we have worked through these values. Taking us out of our comfort zones we tried: salsa dancing (such fun and loved by all) meditating, yoga and sound journeys. We learnt about belief systems through art and drama. For many it has changed their lives not only in the work place but also at home. Please feel free to talk to our staff about this program. We are happy to share our experiences with you.

Fair Trade in Travel

Fair Trade is an equitable partnership between producers, traders, and consumers. It is a growing international movement that works to ensure that low-income artisans and farmers, the majority of whom live in Latin America, Africa, Asia, and the Caribbean, are fairly compensated for their work. Fair Trade marketers in developed countries foster long-term, direct relationships with these small-scale producers, bypassing the world market. As a result of this connection, the producers of Fair Trade products are ensured adequate prices for their goods, independent of current and unpredictable world prices.

Fair Trade wholesalers, retailers, and producers operate in agreement with the following criteria from the Fair Trade Federation (FTF):

- Paying fair wages in local context: workers are fairly compensated for their labor
- Supporting participatory workplaces: smaller cooperatives and producer associations help maintain safe and healthy working conditions, and the producers are better able to control and decide how to distribute their resources.
- Ensuring environmental sustainability: Fair Trade organizations use environmentally sustainable practices to manage local resources.
- Supplying financial and technical support: Fair Trade producers often lack access to affordable financing, so

Fair Trade marketers often provide financial assistance to producers either through direct loans, prepayment, or linking producers with sources of financing.

- Respecting cultural identity: Fair Trade organizations seek to promote producers' artistic talents in a way that preserves cultural identity.
- Offering public accountability: for members of the FTF, finances, management policies, and business practices are open to the public and available for monitoring by the FTF
- Educating consumers: Fair Trade organizations educate consumers on the importance of buying fairly traded products that support healthy working conditions, environmental sustainability, and adequate wages.

Fair Trade in Travel programs create the opportunity for local workers to educate visitors about the benefits of Fair Trade and allow artisans to share their craft. A number of tours are available that encourage a constructive interaction between travelers and the communities they visit. Some programs even offer workshops, where you can learn the trades of your skilled hosts, or volunteer opportunities within the host communities. Personally interacting with these individuals provides a new perspective on the importance of Fair Trade in enabling marginalized producers and workers in developing countries to build a sustainable future for themselves, their families and their communities.

Travelers can easily make a difference by supporting locally owned businesses and visiting local markets. Another way to positively impact a community is to purchase Fair Trade products, available online and in some stores as well as abroad, to help guarantee that the producer receives sufficient compensation for the product or service that they offer.

Explore the World of Fair Trade

General Information

- For more information on the Fair Trade in Travel initiative, visit Sustainable Travel International
- The Fair Trade Federation has guidelines, criteria for Fair Trade businesses and producers, and general information
- The International Federation for Alternative Trade (IFAT) works t o promote Fair Trade while linking Fair Trade associations in Africa, Asia, and Latin America

See for yourself: Fair Trade Trips

These tours provide travelers the opportunity to understand the issues of Fair Trade on a personal level and to experience first-hand how Fair Trade works.

- Pachamama: A World of Artisans, provides tours of several worker-owned cooperatives in Nicaragua.
- Global Exchange offers "Reality Tours." These organized trips allow participants to see adverse situations in other countries firsthand. The Reality Tour options include opportunities to visit and even work with Fair Trade cooperatives.
- ResponsibleTravel.com works in conjunction with many local Fair Trade companies, such as Ajiyer of Bangladesh, People to People Tourism Kenya, and PhunPhiang of Thailand, to name a few. These tours provide the opportunity to meet and even work with local producers all across the world, from Asia, to Africa, to the Caribbean.
- Meet the People tours from Traidcraft let you "meet the people behind the products."
- Fair Trade in Tourism South Africa (FTTSA) offers a variety of accommodations and tours.

Contrary to other Fair Trade offerings, in Fair Trade tourism it is you who travel to the South and spend a time there... not the merchandise. Sometimes one may think that when we travel to exotic places we are somehow helping the people in the country we visit, as we expect that part of the money we spend there will get to them, sooner or later. The reality is that most international tourists who go to developing countries stay at isolated resorts, often owned by foreign corporations, fenced from the locals and only a few of them can profit from that kind of tourism, usually through the tips at the bar. Fortunately, there is a different way of traveling: Fair Trade tourism!

We may consider Fair Trade tourism as a special kind of responsible tourism, in which it is the traveler who gets near the culture and people of the place and tries to get in touch with them, instead of doing it the other way round: having every person involved in tourism conform to western uses.

- ❖ This kind of service is offered by Fair Trade organizations who take advantage of having a lodge (or a network of them) or being situated in any privileged natural location. If you already enjoy any of the available Fair Trade food or other products may be it's the time for a further step.

Ecuador

In this bountiful american country there are two Fair Trade organizations who offer their touristic services. One of them is Grupo Salinas (the photo is theirs); with them you can be at villages as high as 3.500 m above sea level, overlooking magnificient mountains.

- ❖ The other one is Fundación Maquita Cushunchic who can take you through the several landscapes of Ecuador: coast, Andes, Amazonia and Galápagos islands. By the way, they produce the perfumed brown sugar that we sell at Copade World Shop in Madrid, displaying a green andean landscape photo on the package label. Needless to say, it is that sugar what I use at home.

India

If you are interested in visiting Darjeeling "the Fair Trade way", have a look at Makaibari website, as they can offer you staying at an amazing tea estate. It is integrated into a tropical rainforest with a huge diversity of plants and animals.

Malawi

If you are looking for a relaxed accomodation, Satemwa tea estate may be the place for you... or not. You may take part in their tea tasting process, if you wish, or enjoy the nearby sports club available, if you don't. Or visit Thyolo mountain rainforest, if you love Nature, or practice bass fishing at an adjacent lake, if you don't. Or take a mountain bike to ride, if you like action, or just sit at an idyllic scenery point to enjoy a calm sunset, if you don't.

Mozambique

Bespoke experience can offer you staying at their eco-lodges and enjoying scuba diving at Indian Ocean. ... white sand beaches, coral reefs, nice restaurants and the nearby Quirimbas national park can make your holidays unforgettable. A blend of paradise beaches, local culture and wildlife.

Paraguay

There is an association, Estación A which has a branch specialized in touristic activities around lake Yparacaí. Several towns have joined efforts to preserve the monuments of their region and they have created this worthwhile initiative.

Peru

Another andean country which you can visit, Minka Fair Trade has developed a really comprehensive website which details a couple of long (more than two weeks) itineraries covering from natural sea reserves to spanish colonial period cities as well as ancient Inca places, still full of misteries like the Nazca lines. Of course, lake Titicaca (highest of the world) and famous Machu Picchu sacred city are included.

South Africa

If you are interested in traveling to that country, you may have a look at Fair Trade in Tourism South Africa; they offer about 30 different destinations in that country which include being at a Fair Trade wine estate, hiking, riding horses, rowing on boats... even a five star hotel by a yatch marina is listed! Most of the places they suggest are located in outstanding landscapes and may fit any pocket. You can also enjoy a tour through a natural reserve and see the legendary african wildlife: elephants, leopards... and have your dinner under the stars, surrounded by candles. They managed to get a grant from the UK government to develop their own trademark, which now distinguishes their Fair Trade places.

Tourism Marketing

Marketing is a human activity. All the activities of tourism marketing bear a glaring testimony to this fact. In tourism marketing, we deal with mobile, enthusiastic and pleasure-seeking humans. They are on travel sprees. They want to enjoy the nice places of the world! They are efficient (at least during the courses of their journeys), conscious of the environs they visit, always careful about the money they spend, keen to explore and receptive to every phenomenon/product/service that makes comfortable or ecstatic.

We have defined Marketing in this chapter. Let us now define the term Tourism Marketing. According to Krippendorf, "Marketing in tourism is to be understood as the, systematic and co-ordinated execution of business policy by a tourist undertaking, whether private_ or State, owned at local, regional, national and international levels, to achieve the optimal satisfaction of the needs of identifiable consumer groups and in doing so, achieves an appropriate return."

According to Burkart and Medlick, "Tourism marketing activities are systematic and coordinated efforts extended by the National Tourist Organisation and/or tourists at local levels to optimise the satisfaction of tourist groups and individuals in view of sustained tourism growth."

According to A Kumar, "Tourism marketing is the delineation and execution of activities related to tourism their professional planning and execution and finally, ensuring the satisfaction of customers (tourists) in such a manner that the marketing objectives of the tourism organisation are achieved within the framework of social, economic, political and environmental components of the place/region/country of origin as well as that of the place/region/country of tour destination."

Thus, we can arrive at some conclusions regarding tourism marketing, as follows :-

- Tourism marketing is the process of delivering satisfaction to tourists and in this process, the tourism marketer achieve his personal goals or the goals of the firm he works for.
- Tourism marketing is a service-based activity. Some parts of its realm are products, some of them (like food beverages etc.) being very important.
- Just like other types of marketing, tourism marketing also involves:

Strategic Planning (which includes definition of business mission, corporate strategic planning, business strategic planning, goal formulation definition of a marketing plan, finalization of marketing programmes, implementation of marketing programmes and finally, receipt of feedback and control);

Analysis of Marketing Opportunities (which includes marketing research, study of marketing environment, study of consumer behaviour and finally, study of competition);

Selection of Targeted Markets (which includes forecasting market demand, defining market segments, making plans for market targeting and finally, product positioning);

Design of Appropriate Marketing Strategies (which includes definition and identification of market leaders, challengers, followers and niches, defining the PLC of the product and using this knowledge to create market niches for the product/service and finally, understanding the intricacies of import and export management);

Planning Marketing Programmes (which includes definition and management of product lines and brands, development and testing of new products, brand management, marketing of services, pricing policies and discounts, definition and consolidation of marketing channels, study and consolidation of physical distribution channels, making effective promotion strategies, defining sales promotion and public relations programmes and finally, management of the sales force);

Implementing Marketing Programmes (which includes study/creation of a marketing organisation and implementation of marketing programmes in targeted market niches); and.

Controlling (which includes various types of control systems in the parlance of marketing).

- It is a process of transforming potential customers (tourists) into actual customers.
- It is a fine technique for generating and consolidating tourism demand.
- It can be used to increase market share of the tourism marketer.
- It essentially uses the tenets of communication, business management and psychology to win the markets in the parlance of tourism administration.
- It deals with human beings most of the times; they are the customers with very special and weird needs. Most

of them indulge in activities related to tourism due to the fact that they want to enjoy. This peculiar feature of tourism marketing makes it special. It also demands different marketing strategies to woo the customers towards the products and services that are offered to them.

- Tourism packages, Group inclusive Tours, economy package deals and luxury packages area part of the gamut of tourism marketing.
- It involves many services or products of the infrastructure of a region or country. This makes it a Herculean effort; without making right types of teams, a tourism marketer cannot succeed in this effort.
- Tourism marketing starts from implementation of local or regional programmes but eventually, all the marketers try (or dream) to win international market hitches which were hitherto beyond their reach.

Tourism is predominantly a service. It involves many people (tourists, tour operators, transporters, hotel staff, guides, restaurant staff, disk jockeys etc.). It is of perishable nature.

The unique features of tourism demand are as follows :-

- It is perishable by nature.
- The demand is more during peak seasons and very low during off seasons.
- Tourists demand products and services of different kinds from the producers of the same set of tourism services or products. But they have to produce all such types of these services or product to remain competitive in the markets.
- Demand for luxury products and services is low. Demand for low-end services and product is very high.
- Some tourists, who may be belonging to middle-income strata of the society, may try to touch, albeit occasionally, the luxury norms of the strata that are above their strata.

- For some tourist spots, the demand is more or less inelastic. But for others, it is elastic.

As already stated, tourism is a service. It comprises some products as well. These include food, liquor, beverages, gifts, souvenirs, items, of daily use etc. But basically, the tourist (customer) buys services while he takes up a tour or itinerary. Example: One cannot expect a tourist to go to Mauritius to buy a few items that are typical to that country. He travels to that country to enjoy her environs, swim in the blue waters of the ocean, stay at exotic places and have a glimpse of the coral reefs that are under the waters of the ocean. He may or may not buy gifts or souvenirs, though he would certainly eat the cuisine of Mauritius.

Now that we are clear about the tenet that tourism is a service, we would have to weave a strategy set to bring customers to our fold. Service marketing is different from product marketing. It is intangible; the tourist cannot consume a tourist spot can only enjoy its environs. When he goes back to his native place, he takes sweet memories along with him. The tourism product is, therefore, essentially associated with 3 features, as follows: -

- Perceptions in the mind of the tourist-to-be about the tourist spot, including his expectations and a portrayal of what is in store for him.
- The actual experiences (good or bad) of the tourist at the spot.
- Sweet memories (even bitter ones) that he takes back along with him to his native place.

If a customer tries a product and does not like it, he discards it. But if a tourist tries a tourist spot and does not like it, he cannot cancel his tour. This feature differentiates tourism (as a service) from other services and products. He cannot call it a day in the middle of the journey because he was offered beef and pork by the hotel! He has to drag on somehow. Our advice to the tourism marketer is-do not let the tourist have the feeling of dragging on; eliminate this feeling as soon as it develops in his mind. If you don't, he would not give a good word-of-mouth about your tourist spot or service to others. You would lose him as well as scores of other tourists who could have become your customers, had he been treated nicely to kill that feeling of dragging on.

Further, tourism, as a service, is given only when political stability of the region is ensured.

Instance: Kashmir is a paradise on the earth but not a hot spot for tourists because of the supremacy of terrorists in that valley. A tourist does not like the hullabaloo of crowd, rallies, riots, arson and instability. He wants to enjoy and relax at the tourist spot; he may have spent the savings of his return to undertake the trip. Every tourism organisation must understand this fact.

Salient Features

The following features are important :-

- Tourism marketing activities are executed at regional, national and international levels.
- It leads to creation of a service or set of services. Some products are also included in its gamut but the "service aspect" of this gargantuan field is more important.
- It is a managerial process and is designed to earn profits for the tourism marketing firm or the producer who manufactures products/services related to tourism.
- The basic tenet of tourism marketing is the satisfaction of needs of tourists (or would-be tourists).
- New products/services can be created and marketed from a scratch and also, old products/services can be marketed/sold to customers.
- The nature of tourism product/service is perishable. Hence, tourism marketers are always on their toes to market these products/services to the prospective buyers so that marketers are able to sell as much of these within the given time frames.

- Just like they try to do in other marketing programmes, tourism marketers try to create new users, convert light users into medium users and convert medium users into heavy users.
- Links of tourism marketers are at regional, national and global levels. They cannot survive in the markets without associating with their counterparts in other regions of the world. They have to depend, unlike conventional marketers, on such persons or firms for ensuring that their clients (tourists) get the coveted sets of products/services. Thus, distribution of the product or service is done by many players, each one of them claiming a small share in the profit cake. In conventional marketing, the distribution channels take a share of profits after the sale has been effected. In tourism marketing, various components of tourism get their respective shares in advance. Example: The airline, hotel, local transporter etc. get their amounts in advance. Shopping is done by the tourist either through a credit card or by paying cash at the counter. Other hotel expenses like bar, restaurant are paid for by the tourist when he checks out of the hotel. In some cases, tickets to various forts, palaces, parks etc. are to be purchased by the tourist at such spots. Hence, some components of the itinerary are prepaid while some other have to be paid for at the time of purchasing those components. Thus, the system of extending credit does not exist in tourism marketing, especially in international tourism marketing. There are 3 exceptions to this rule. Firstly, in the operations of time share resorts, tourists-to-be because members and use the tourist spot for a limited number of days. They pay some amount in advance and pay the balance in convenient installments. Secondly, some tourists may take loans from banks and private lenders and pay back to them after they have completed the tours. In the second case, the payments are made to tour operators in advance. Thirdly, some tour

operators have also started extending credit facilities to tourists; they charge interest and deliver services related to transport, accommodation and leisure before actually receiving the payments. However in general, the tourism industry is the "first pay avail later" type of industry.

- Tourists have to be guided throughout the course of an itinerary. That is because they' are new to the tourist spot. Language, cultural differences and individual motivation are some of the factors that affect their actions and desires lour guides, hotel staff, transporters and operative staff at fun parks, theme parks and other places of leisure help these tourists so that they could enjoy their stints at such places. So, tourism marketing does not end with sale of tickets or booking of hotel rooms. It must be executed in a professional manner till the last phase of the tour itinerary.
- As already stated, differences in life-styles, languages, cultures, cuisine, daily habits religions and perceptions (of tourists) force marketers to adopt varying strategies during the course of an itinerary. Each one of tourists ought to be looked after in a different manner. In the parlance of Group Inclusive Tours (GITs), individual attention cannot be given. But in individual and family tours, the needs of an individual or a family can be addressed with professional finesse. However, GITs are cheap and individual/family tours (or those that are organised according to special programmers) are very costly.
- Production and consumption of tourism services are closely interrelated. Most of the tourism services cannot be consumed incrementally. So, consumption, once started, cannot be stopped are modified. So, risk or uncertainty is higher for the customer. So, he seeks precise information sets or data before he undertakes a tour. He cannot see, feel, touch or inspect the services/ products related to tourism before he decides to use

them. But he can make comparisons of services offered by different competitors, namely, resorts, airlines, hotels, bars, discotheques etc. But here lies the crux of the problem. He does not know much (or anything) about the tourist place he intends to visit. He can only use a few criteria, namely, grade of the hotel, location of the hotel, class of airline (executive, royal executive, economy etc.), duration of the tour, reputation of the travel agency and image of the tourist spot! country, to take a decision. When he actually goes through the tour, then only he realises what were the wrong decisions in his selection.

- Different manufacturers join hands to form a tourism product. An airline considers seats flown or passenger miles covered as its product. A hotel produces guest nights. A theatre considers the number of visitors as its product. All these components form a whole that we call Tourism Product. As already stated, services form a major part of this product. Marketing efforts are needed not only to sell all these components as a whole, but also to execute these components when the tourist places an order to buy the package. Once an order has been placed (and money received), neither the buyer nor the seller can withdraw from the contract. Products and services cannot be rejected in tourism. However, these can be modified (at a cost to the customer) but within the limits imposed by the itinerary, various producers of products and services, law of the land and financial resources of the customer (tourist).
- Tourism demand is unstable. It depends upon seasons political upheavals, wars, modes of transport, accessibility to the tourist spot, financial resources of the customer (tourist), currency fluctuations, international relations force mejeure' etc.
- Travel motivations are diverse in nature. Different people take up tours for different reasons.

Instance: For the youth, fun could be the criterion to visit London. But for an old couple, ancient monuments, the Big Ben and Stonehenge could be the places to be visited (and not fun parks and night life). Humans are different in terms of motivations, perceptions and actions. So, they ought to be treated as individuals. Tour programmers are costly. Individual tour programmes are much more costlier than GITs. The marketer must, therefore, identify some common motivations of the tourist group. He should segregate customers on the basis of these travel motivations. It would be easier for him to understand their precise needs and serve them.

Tourism Marketing Skills

The staff engaged in various occupations must be trained to satisfy their valued customers. Further, education alone would not be sufficient in the gargantuan field of tourism administration. The marketing staff would have to gain useful and productive experience too. In this section, we shall briefly describe some marketing skills that would have to be developed/mastered by the marketing and execution staff of the tourism industry.

If a firm/hotel/travel agency is creative and innovative, it can get a regular stream of orders. Similarly, if the staff of a firm engaged in the tourism business (public or private) are creative, their employers are certainly likely to gain. Brand image is improved and cash counters sales increase if creative forces of the organisation are put to use.

According to John F Mea, "Creative thinking is the process of bringing a problem before one's mind clearly as by imaging, visualising, supposing, musing, contemplating or the like and then, originating an idea/concept, realisation or picture along new or unconventional lines. It involves study and reflection rather than action."

There are 5 stages in the creative process, as follows: -

- Saturation.
- Preparation.

- Incubation.
- Illumination.
- Verification.

The concepts of havelis, farm tourism, eco tourism and adventure tourism were the outputs of creative brains. The marketers designed old havelis as new destinations and added a touch of ethnicity to these settings/premises of the yore. And the results were quite encouraging. Similarly, Palace on Wheels, Royal Orient, Euro Rail, Amtrak, Star Cruises and Frequent Flier Programme (of the IA) are the living examples of creativity of a handful of people. If creativity were eliminated from the arena of tourism, we would not find any customers in this field. Creative design patterns and art objects of the yore attract the attention of mullions. So, tourists long for a creative touch in everything they buy, eat, drink, see or enjoy. They want to switch off the routine; and a tour is an ideal concept to break free. If this concept is given inputs of creativity, the tourists may not leave the tourist spots but stay there forever.

Language based Communication : All the persons involved in the travel and tourism trade ought to learn at least three languages. These are the mother tongue, the national language and at least one international language. They must also learn to empathise with tourists, visitors or hotel guests. Polite speech, decent body language and suave personality are the vital elements that make a person a successful seller. Letters, fax messages and E-mail messages must be written dearly and also, sent in time. Courtesy calls must also be made in this field.

The person must allow the visitor to speak. If language is a barrier the travel agent should show some standard pictures (e.g, Car, Food, Hungry, Thirsty, Going, Coming, I Cannot, I Can, Train, Airline, Ticket, Coach, Water, Wine, Doctor, Police etc) to the tourist so that he may be able to express his need. Documents related to travel or stay must be neatly typed. Advertisements should be in a language that the targeted customers understand with ease.

Self-motivation Staff : The staff engaged in various sectors of tourism a must be self-motivated to work and deliver concrete results. Motivation and morale are closely related. If a person's morale were high, he would be motivated to work and give sterling performances. If his morale were low, he would not give good performances at all. People are motivated by different factors; such factors would also combine with their mental make-up, backgrounds, education, family status, economic conditions etc. The management has to identity the chief motivating factors for a person. Accordingly, it must define a set of motivating factors for each person instead of treating them with the same set of such factors. This person-to-person treatment would develop the organisation.

CHAPTER-12

TOURISM, SMALL ENTERPRISES AND COMMUNITY DEVELOPMENT

Tourism Enterprises has been designed to provide you with a broad understanding of business operations within a tourism organisation. This specialty has been set up as a project - you get to start up and run your own bed and breakfast establishment. During your journey you will look at marketing, financial planning, managerial skills, recruitment, and operating and information systems requirements.

Small and medium enterprises (also SMEs, small and medium businesses, SMBs, and variations thereof) are companies whose headcount or turnover falls below certain limits.

The abbreviation SME occurs commonly in the European Union and in international organizations, such as the World Bank, the United Nations and the WTO. The term small and medium businesses or SMBs is predominantly used in the USA.

EU Member States traditionally have their own definition of what constitutes an SME, for example the traditional definition in Germany had a limit of 250 employees, while, for example, in Belgium it could have been 100. But now the EU has started to standardize the concept. Its current definition categorizes companies with fewer than 10 employees as "micro", those with fewer than 50 employees as "small", and those with fewer than

250 as "medium". By contrast, in the United States, when small business is defined by the number of employees, it often refers to those with fewer than 100 employees, while medium-sized business often refers to those with fewer than 500 employees. Both the US and the EU generally use the same threshold of fewer than 10 employees for small offices (SOHO).

In most economies, smaller enterprises are much greater in number. In the EU, SMEs comprise approximately 99% of all firms and employ between them about 65 million people. In many sectors, SMEs are also responsible for driving innovation and competition. Globally SMEs account for 99% of business numbers and 40% to 50% of GDP.

In India, the Micro and Small Enterprises (MSEs) sector plays a pivotal role in the overall industrial economy of the country. It is estimated that in terms of value, the sector accounts for about 39% of the manufacturing output and around 33% of the total export of the country. Further, in recent years the MSE sector has consistently registered higher growth rate compared to the overall industrial sector. The major advantage of the sector is its employment potential at low capital cost. As per available statistics, this sector employs an estimated 31 million persons spread over 12.8 million enterprises and the labour intensity in the MSE sector is estimated to be almost 4 times higher than the large enterprises.

In South Africa the term is SMME for Small, Medium and Micro Enterprises. Elsewhere in Africa, MSME is used for Micro, Small and Medium Enterprises.

Industry Canada defines a small business as one that has fewer than 100 employees (if the business is a goods-producing business) or fewer than 50 employees (if the business is a service-based business), and a medium-sized business as fewer than 500. In New Zealand a SME has to be 19 people or fewer.

The growing interest in community tourism development is paralleled within the European Union by a switch of emphasis away from large automatic grants to attract inward investment projects, towards small firms, and indigenous development. The promotion of small and medium enterprises by the union is on the basis that these firms provide the community underpinnings for entrepreneurship and job creation. Taking the experience of Wales as an example, the full-time equivalent employment out-turns from 216 projects are analyzed to assess job creation performance against targets. On the whole, the small and medium tourism enterprises in question were either in line with or better than their employment targets.

Promoting Broad-Based Sustainable Development Through Tourism

Problems

Early tourism development has given little consideration to natural resource limitations, impacts on wildlife and indigenous cultures. The human environment and development has been largely ignored. Within the process of globalisation local communities' participation and nature conservation are threatened and often overlooked.

If tourism is to be sustainable, it must improve the lives of local people, protect their environment and health and offer a better future. In many instances tourism can be seen as a vehicle to empower local communities and protect the environment through the development of new employment opportunities, the enhancement of local economies, preservation of indigenous knowledge and practices, public awareness and education.

Sustainable tourism can create positive opportunities for community development in remote areas. The business sector can choose sustainable tourism over other more polluting ventures. Long and short term development plans should be developed so that tourism and its benefits are spread within the area. To develop tourism in a sustainable manner it is necessary to define optimal tourism destinations in local areas and regions, ensuring enjoyment for the tourist and minimum impact or disruption for the environment and local communities.

Complex and broad based local communities' involvement in tourism development requires targeted investment strategies implemented by local decision-makers. Those strategies do not exist in many areas and the development of tourism is not planned. Tourism investments are too often imposed from the outside, and the potential for sustainable forms of tourism is weakened. Alternatives to mass tourism, eg cultural and ecotourism, can be influential in changing the nature of tourism. Tourism can benefit both tourists and local communities and allow for two-way interaction and education.

Solutions

In order for tourism to become a sustainable industry, countries, states, regions, and individuals must work with new technology, natural resource management and marketing concepts. Ideally, participatory planning and implementation will be a part of Local Agenda 21 processes. To ensure community involvement and to safeguard local cultures, sustainable tourism development should therefore involve all stakeholders in tourism development at all appropriate levels, facilitate the development of tourism services that are planned, managed and reviewed by the host community in Local Agenda 21 processes, ensure that tourism revenue stays in the host communities to enhance livelihoods and generate a profitable source of income, empower and motivate local groups to direct cross-cultural exchange in the way they wish and adopt practices which conserve, protect and preserve the environment.

Local and regional Tourism Boards should be created, involving all stakeholders. These Boards should:

- promote sustainable tourism concepts in co-operation with local governments and all stakeholders, in line with Local Agenda 21 priorities;
- work systematically to attract investment in sustainable tourism;
- help other institutions in developing marketing strategies and training programmes and developing educational materials;

- work together with different public institutions to involve all stakeholder groups in tourism activities, and bring greater benefits to the entire community;
- co-operate with grass-roots organisations to develop employment strategies through sustainable tourism.

Institutional Action

The UN-CSD should:

- invite countries to integrate tourism into their sustainable development strategies for the 2002 review;
- ask the review progress in local communities involvement in tourism development in their country profiles to the preparatory meetings for Earth Summit III in 2002 as part of the review process;
- instruct DESA in cooperation with relevant UN agencies and convention secretariats, major groups and all stakeholders to develop indicators of sustainable tourism;
- invite convention secretariats and the Committee on the Environment of the WTO-OMC to report annually to the CSD;
- establish an international ombuds office to deal with human rights abuses and environmental destruction in tourism;.
- ask UNEP through their Industry Office to work with industry associations at all levels, trade unions, local authorities and NGOs to develop a framework for 'good practice' and to develop a database on good practice, criteria, examples and analysis which should be accessible to governments and stakeholders alike;
- ask UNEP together with UNCHS, the Sustainable Cities Programme and relevant stakeholders to develop guidance notes on tourism within Local Agenda 21.
- ask the UN Regional Commissions to prepare a report for the preparatory meetings for Earth Summit III in

2002 on sustainable and community-based tourism activities within their region and to work with UNEP/WTO to develop regional agreements to address sustainable tourism.

- invite UNDP to share its work on guidelines for "good practice" and to involve indigenous peoples and local communities this work;
- ask the UNDP country offices to bring together UN agencies, bilateral donors and other stakeholders to work together on sustainable tourism, involving the gender development programme in this process;
- ask UNDP to include sustainable tourism into its poverty alleviation strategies and programmes.
- ask the United Nations Commission on Trade and Development to integrate tourism into their development strategies and include a progress review on the role of indigenous and local communities' involvement in tourism for the Earth Summit III (year 2002) review and to support community-owned and controlled initiatives in tourism and biodiversity through its BIOTRADE initiative.
- invite environmental conventions and treaties secretariats to include community-based tourism in their action plans and programmes and to promote it as an incentive for the conservation and sustainable use of biodiversity.

Multilateral financing and assistance agencies should:

- provide funds for applied research through pilot projects to determine optimal mechanisms for tourism development in a range of differing circumstances;
- create small-scale credit lines to assist small enterprises to invest in tourism without excessive risk on personal property;
- support community controlled tourism initiatives that are directed to poverty alleviation, biodiversity conservation and promotion of human rights;

- assess their projects' effectiveness on local, sub-national and national levels involving all stakeholders and publish the results by the Earth Summit III in 2002;
- take part in a discussion forum on minimising leakage, with findings to be brought back to the finance discussion at CSD-8 in 2000. Possible outcomes include the development of a purchasing/procurement strategy for the tourism industry, local/ national investment strategies, improved mechanisms for informed choice by consumers, and a linking of aid with capacity building in tourism-dependent areas.

Governments Should

At national level:

- establish/clarify institutional and departmental responsibility for developing outgoing tourism and harmonise institutional interventions;
- initiate the use of tourism for local economic development by involving all sectors alongside the tourist ministry; to build the capacity to work at the destination level, including product development and effective management of existing destinations;
- facilitate research grants on sustainable tourism, methodologies, impacts and analysis of good practice; finance pilot schemes to develop 'good practice' and establish systems for ongoing evaluation and monitoring;
- establish sustainable tourism policies and regulations, ensuring responsibly zoned development; natural and cultural heritage and resource conservation and protection;
- review land ownership in potential tourism areas and where possible transfer ownership to local communities and provide the necessary training for them;
- include the perspective of local and indigenous communities into local and national sustainable development strategies;

- increase funding for local NGOs to enable them to engage in a dialogue on tourism;
- support public education programmes which encourage responsible consumption, natural resource use, environmental protection and local culture conservation;
- give priority to the following investment suggestions: create funds to help tour operators improve their technical capacity for sustainable tourism development; create funds to develop recreational facilities for the public;
- encourage local banks and other lending institutions to set up regional investment funding programmes, including micro-credit programmes;
- create Regional Tourism Boards, fully staffed, to help in planning, promoting, regulating, and expanding sustainable tourism; initiate special marketing programmes by local governments and Tourism Boards, in which local tourism programmes will be advertised in the media; initiate programmes to improve the management of ecotourism in protected areas; set up training programmes for guides, tour operators, marketers, etc.

At local level:

- harmonise laws on tourism including regulations, fee standards, licensing, etc. so that they will be more favourable to sustainable tourism in the region;
- ensure that tourism development is in line with Local Agenda 21 priorities and land-use plans and that the public can participate in local and regional decision making;
- regulate tourism to ensure that profits benefit local people and conservation efforts;
- develop and support programmes to revitalise the diverse aspects of local cultures.

The tourism industry should:

- reduce financial leakage and support local economies by buying food and resources locally, develop long-term partnerships with local operators, businesses and suppliers; train and hire local staff and contract with local businesses, promote management opportunities for women; prefer accommodations owned, built and staffed by local people, promote locally made handicrafts and traditional products;
- encourage clients to study and understand their destinations, respect local cultures and co-ordinate visits with local communities, authorities and women's organisations, being aware of and sensitive to local customary laws, regulations and traditions, respect historical heritage and scientific sites;
- educate staff to avoid negative environmental and cultural impacts and create incentive schemes to promote sustainable behaviour.

NGOs should:

- initiate stakeholder dialogue on community involvement in tourism development, recognising social and gender divisions in communities;
- promote consultation processes in tourism planning, involving local communities;
- launch educational and awareness programmes on tourism for local communities, support and promote history research and museums;
- promote the respect for indigenous peoples and local communities' self-determination, autonomy and social and cultural integrity;
- strengthen their efforts to empower disenfranchised groups (in particular women) to become involved in local tourism planning and management;
- develop participatory programmes to support the integrity of local cultures and economies;

- support the sustainable resource use and initiate environmental actions on different levels to conserve the environment while the tourism is developing;
- analyse the experience with sustainable tourism in different parts of the world to disseminate methodology/positive examples of community involvement in tourism;
- support the use of traditional knowledge, practices and innovation systems relevant for the conservation and sustainable use of biological resources and promote actions on different levels to eradicate poverty, protect human rights and conserve the environment while working in tourism.

Possible Partnerships

There is an urgency to constructively shape tourism in order to support local development and conservation goals. UN bodies and institutions, governments, industry and civil society should co-operate to launch a dialogue process on sustainable tourism. This must be planned within the framework provided by the various UN treaties and declarations. All the stakeholders involved in and affected by tourism should be involved in the development of action plans for sustainable tourism. Identifying mechanisms to achieve sustainable development goals in tourism must be a priority for co-operation. 'Good practices' in conserving culture and nature while developing sustainable tourism should be collected world-wide, involving all stakeholders. This process should lead to a multi-stakeholder round-table on strategic planning of local community involvement in tourism to be organised by UNEP as a side event at the Preparatory meetings for Earth Summit III in 2002.

There is an urgent need to assess the impacts of globalisation and the role of multilateral and bilateral development organisations in unsustainable tourism practices. An independent international assessment commission should be created under the CSD. NGOs, indigenous peoples, women's organisations and local communities should be involved in this assessment process together with all other stakeholders. The UN Working Group on Indigenous Peoples should be invited to monitor impacts of tourism on indigenous peoples and local communities. The assessment is to be completed and published by the year 2002.

Maine Tourism Marketing Partnership Program

The Maine Tourism Marketing Partnership Program (MTMPP), sponsored by Maine's DECD's Office of Tourism, provides grants for small businesses that "create and implement programs designed to stimulate and expand the tourism," according to the Office of Tourism website. Grants are awarded to just a handful of applicants. The MTMPP recommends calling 207-624-9808 for more information.

Environment and Agriculture

In rural and marginalized areas the majority of the population works in agriculture. Often the prices they receive from the selling of their crops are extremely low and do not satisfy human development needs. In a competitive market with many people selling the same products it becomes neccesarry to find niche crops and improve agricultural practices to deliver more of a sustainable income to farmers. Also, with an increasing population it is crucial to find a balance between agricultural needs and the fragile Ecuadorian environment.

Cacao: Yanapuma Foundation works towards the promotion and formation of cacao promoters and cacao associations. In this process we work with local counterparts and beneficiaries to improve and make more sustainable their production methods with the future objective of commercialization for sale to fair trade, organic, and similar markets. The overall long- term goal is to sell this cacao to an international market where chocolate could than be produced, or go one step further and begin local production of chocolate for sale nationally and internationally.

Sustainable agriculture: Yanapuma foundation aims to implement sustainable agricultural practices, minimizing theuse of harmful chemical products and farming methods and promoting the growing of organic crops. With prices at extremely low levels due to the nature of the market in Ecuador many agriculturalists barely make enough to get by. Yanapuma works with local beneficiaries to begin to improve production methods in order to receive a higher price in the national and international market. The overall objective is to promote a form of agriculture that does not use dangerous pesticides, works in concert with the environment and delivers a more just return for local agriculturalists.

Conservation: Ecuador is a country of extreme bio-diversity but also the country with the highest population density in Latin America. The achievement of a balance between this bio-diversity and the increasing population is of extreme importance for not only the future of Ecuador but the world.

Reforestation: Yanapuma foundation believes in the importance of a balance between agriculture and the environment. To this end reforestation is a crucial component of the conservation of what already exists and indeed the creation of spaces for a future, long-term balance to begin to take shape. We work with local beneficiaries to grow native tree species and then plant these trees to begin to reforest around agricultural areas as well as near rivers to protect water courses. We also work in local schools to demonstrate the importance of conservation, reforestation and general respect for plants, animals and the environment in general.

Appropriate technology: Yanapuma foundation, in collaboration with local counterparts, works in the development and promotion of appropriate technology to satisfy water and sanitation needs. Working with local people Yanapuma helps to design and implement the construction of ecological toilets, which conserve water and provide fertilizer for growing nutritious crops and plants. We also work with schools in the construction of worm farms that use their organic waste and composting bins to provide fertilizer, helping to educate children about the differences between organic and inorganic waste.

Health and Well-being

In rural and marginalized areas of Ecuador health services are often extremely limited. The government is often unable to provide basic care for these people. Although there is often some medicine available for people there is almost a complete lack of preventative education. This leads to huge costs for curing illnesses when these costs could be removed by providing the capacity to prevent illness and disease before they occur.

Integrated health promotion: The Yanapuma Foundation aims to facilitate integrated health promotion through the formation of local health promoters in collaboration with regional health service organizations. This includes capacity development in preventive health practices such as primary care, nutrition, maternal care and safe water consumption. We also work to provide a space for the use of indigenous medicinal plants and methods alongside Western medicine practices. The objective of integrated health promotion is to improve well-being and promote a vision of health as holistic and participatory

Economic Opportunity

With the extremely low return from traditional agricultural methods and other forms of employment, rural and marginalized areas often find it very difficult to improve their economic situation. Because of this situation, innovative forms of economic opportunity need to be put into action. In Ecuador there is a growing market for community tourism and indigenous craft production. Also, the formation of small enterprises allows for local people to use their agricultural knowledge, cultural heritage and artisan skills to tap into local and national capital markets.

Yanapuma works with rural and marginalized communities in the formation of small enterprises and their integration into increasingly profitable markets, concentrating on community tourism, craft production and niche products. By providing the training and technical assistance and facilitating access to capital and market linkages Yanapuma aims to help small producers and entrepreneurs maximize market opportunities. Yanapuma helps farmers and community members organize themselves in associations and cooperatives, approaching farming, tourism and craft production as a business and giving them the necessary tools to move across the entire value chain; from production and processing to marketing and financing.

Crafts Production

Yanapuma foundation, in collaboration with local counterparts, promotes the organization and legalization of crafts organizations. The foundation works to promote sound business practices and organizational development within these groups to lay the foundation for the growth of a sustainable and profitable business that benefits the needs of the community as a whole.

Sustainable Tourism

Yanapuma foundation, in collaboration with local counterparts, promotes the capacity of communities to implement small scale/low impact sustainable community based tourism projects, which use the natural and cultural resources of a community for the benefit of the community as well as the environment.

Agribusiness

Yanapuma takes a comprehensive approach to developing agricultural businesses across the entire value chain from production and organization to commercialization and marketing. Presently we are working with a cocoa group in Búa de Los Tsáchilas and are improving production and technical capacity as well as finding ways to integrate the group into national cacao markets. Yanapuma is also developing the capacity of small native tree nurseries that will provide alternative sources of income for local beneficiaries. Yanapuma believes that agricultural businesses must work in tandem with the environment at the same time as delivering an improved economic return.

Education and Capacity Development

Yanapuma Foundation believes that the sustainability of development interventions comes from the organization and capacity of the people themselves to continue to run the projects without the presence of the foundation. This necessitates a continual presence in the community working with motivated actors to realize the necessary building blocks for program development, implementation as well as monitoring and evaluation.

Capacity development exercises: In all of our projects we promote the organization of action groups with the capacity to lead and drive projects. By not only developing their capacity to plan and organize we also strive to have these promoters develop the capacity of others so that there is a continual formation and solidification of the basic building blocks to motivate future project development.

Education Curriculum Improvement: Yanapuma Foundation, in collaboration with local counterparts, continually aims to use the local school as a space for learning and dialogue with professors, community members and school children. We believe that change must come from the next generation in order for communities to be truly sustainable. With this long-term view we seek to build an educational environment that is truly context specific and based upon the belief that only through citizen engagement can change processes begin. To this end, we teach English and environmental education as well as work to make the curriculum more context specific in various rural primary schools.

CHATER-13

UNDERSTANDING COMMUNITY TOURISM ENTERPRENEURS

Somewhere centuries ago a community decided to celebrate, and a festival was born. Vendors sensed that people would gather and be in a mood to buy their wares. Townsfolk realized that visitors from afar would need places to rest. Someone knew enough to organize the event and, if that person was a visionary, he knew that revelers would pay to watch the sun go down, that is if accompanying food and music were provided.

Visitors beat new paths to the community. Paths turned into roads. Vendors decided that the festival was sustainable, so they stayed on, calling the place where they gathered to do business the market. The community now had a commercial center. Dwellings that offered hospitality became inns and eating-places. The sun was reliable in its setting. This was the place where tourism was born.

The model described has not changed over time. It is a simple model of tourism development. Add the production of the goods that the vendors offer for sale; then create a strategy for community development that includes local manufacturing; and the process of economic development, as we know it today, becomes definitive.

Tourism developers are marketers. The elements of their marketing activities include recruiting, as well as the creation of products that entice visitors to linger and seek leisure activities that will part them from their money. For all practical purposes, tourism development and tourism promotion are the same things. Promotion is an element of marketing.

Economic developers are marketers also. In areas of the world where the Industrial Age has ended, there is only a semantic distinction between tourism developers and economic developers, in terms of how they function to serve prospects. In fact, industrial developers in North America only began to change their identity to "economic developers" about 25 years ago. Most people worldwide still think of economic development in terms of industrial development.

Economic developers oriented towards industrial development often refer to themselves as community developers when they are engaged in activities related to building local infrastructure. Economic developers often refer to themselves as product developers when they are oriented towards tourism development and similarly engaged in readying their communities. Separating economic development activities into "industrial" or "tourism" is of little importance until it causes confusion for those who own opportunities and have decisions to make that affect locations or expansions and start-ups. The smaller the community, the more important it is that the local economic developer be capable of addressing the needs of all types of prospects.

Entrepreneurs are more likely to be involved in tourism-related product development than are corporate executives responsible for relocating or expanding operations. Entrepreneurs are also more likely to be unfamiliar with the nuances of the economic development process as it relates to finding resources and assistance. In addition to entrepreneurs, investors and property or project developers are generally what make up a "whole" tourism-related prospect.

During the times of industrial development opportunity, communities promote and recruit for prospects that come neatly prepackaged, as compared to times of development opportunity for tourism product, which are primarily commercial opportunities. Industrial prospects generally challenge a community with a standardized set of criteria that place it in a competitive position against other communities. Commercial prospects generally challenge a community to produce evidence of market potential. In essence, a community competes with itself in commercial development. If entrepreneurs seek assistance from economic developers, it is generally because they want help in putting their packages together so that they can become a whole prospect. When they call upon economic developers they often want assistance in finding sources of capital (investors) and people who can make a concept work (developers).

In order to find a starting point for guiding those who want to maintain their communities in a position to grow as commercial centers, as well as for guiding those who are business leaders with opportunities to bring to communities, I wrote this paper as a recap of what I recently learned about tourism product. The time of my learning surrounds the 1996 Summer Olympic Games, which took place in Atlanta, Georgia, USA. The "Atlanta Olympics" was my opportunity to be exposed to all facets of tourism-related product at one time. It was a time in my career as an economic developer when I participated in the greatest variety of projects. I was on the scene before, during and after the event as a consultant with product development responsibilities that extended beyond the metropolitan area of Atlanta throughout the state of Georgia, and into the whole region of the Southeastern United States as well. I was involved with prospects interested in capturing the market created by the event in Atlanta, as well as prospects interested in developing permanent markets in rural areas. I was forced to define tourism product and carefully consider its process when confronted with any opportunity that would affect its development.

WHAT IS PRODUCT DEVELOPMENT?

All of the definitions of tourism-related product that I have yet heard have an obvious common thread. A promotional brochure has been defined to me as product. An event, such as a family reunion, has been described to me as product. Organizing tours to give city people an opportunity to experience rural life is regularly suggested at tourism conferences as a product worthy of development. The common thread woven through all of these points is that product must appeal to travelers and people seeking leisure-time activities.

Alvin Rosenbaum of the National Center for Heritage Development (formerly the National Coalition for Heritage Areas) said, "Tourism product supported by public agencies is a blend of conservation, community and economic development." He said this at the annual meeting of the American Association of Museums in 1997.

Earlier at a Cultural Tourism Leadership Forum in Chapel Hill, North Carolina, Jerold Kappel raised the issue of how to define product. Mr. Kappel, who is the American Association of Museums' (AAM) director of development, included a need to interpret what product is among five challenges to its development. In later correspondence to my wife and business partner he explained and emphasized the importance of considering product development within the context of the whole community. He wrote that tourism product is community-based. He wrote, "...what makes cultural tourism unique is that people go to absorb and experience the culture of a place." He earlier defined "place" as a destination with a story to tell to a visitor.

Both the imaginary model that introduces this paper and the Atlanta Olympics model can be identified as "market models." The first was presented as a permanent market that formed from an event. The latter was an established market that was enhanced by an event. Market is critical to product development. In Atlanta, it was necessary to build a sports infrastructure to support the Olympics. The right product in the right place, at the right time, is critical to turning a commercial development opportunity into a reality.

Prior to the 1996 Summer Olympic games, Atlanta developed an infrastructure to appeal to sports fans. That infrastructure was tested for its market potential, long before the Olympics came along. The state provided the city with a conference and trade show center that was the foundation for building an infrastructure to accommodate the business traveler. The movie, Gone With The Wind, gave Atlanta its major historic theme, and support from people who made money from successful Atlanta based businesses such as Coca-Cola helped build a foundation for its appeal to visitors with cultural interests.

If you analyze Atlanta from a historic point of view, you arrive at a point in time when there was a rural community in its place. If you analyze Atlanta from a cultural point of view, you see that, at exactly the right time in its development, it embraced all the elements of its culture and heritage.

Landmark Event

If you analyze Atlanta from the standpoint of its most recent landmark event in tourism development, the 1996 Summer Olympic Games, you see that its cultural and heritage position had to be established ahead of time. The fact that an infrastructure for sports-related tourism had to be created in recent times is more obvious than the fact that government and business working together in partnership was the key to making the event, itself, successful in its chosen location.

Atlanta and the State of Georgia, including its influential economic development allies, made assumptions about tourism and economic development ahead of the 1996 Summer Olympics Games. Programs were developed around these assumptions and a lot of money spent. Unfortunately, there was little direct economic development return to the city and, especially, the state. This would be difficult to prove, however, due to the fact that a winner's spin was put on reporting so that investors in the programs could feel good about them. This paper was not written to address negative issues regarding the matter, but its author feels that facing up to failure is the right thing to do so that experience can be gained - and passed on.

Scaling the Atlanta Olympics model back in its application as a model for even a small, rural community, makes a clear case for establishing a tourism market based on heritage and cultural appeal. Consider the fact that Atlanta's Olympic heritage is now a part of its history.

At the beginning of the third chapter, "Product Development: Increasing Attractiveness to Tourists," of her book, Partnerships for Prosperity Museums and Economic Development, Dr. Peggy Wireman wrote these words: "From the point of view of economic development, a museum is a product - something that attracts visitors ..."

Traditional Museums

Relatively few traditional museums are operated as "for-profit" enterprises; nevertheless, they are important as economic development entities that complete the formula for success in attracting visitors to most communities. Dr. Wireman's definition of product from the cultural and heritage point of view, coupled with Mr. Kappel's suggestion that product is a place of interest to tourists, helps underscore what my imaginary model is meant to convey the whole community must be given consideration as a product to develop. Consider the fact that Walt Disney World is a master-planned community, designed as a whole, to be nothing more than a tourist attraction. There are many facets to its success, not the least of which is its unified presentation as a community.

Using what I learned from Dr. Wireman and Mr. Kappel, I stress another important point that is directly aimed at the practice of economic development. Practitioners, professional and volunteers alike, must be willing to take on projects for not-for-profit cultural and heritage-related operations, such as museums, if they are to play a role in preparing their communities to attract visitors.

My point is strengthened by the example of the site selection project for the Mighty Eighth Air Force Heritage Museum near Savannah, Georgia. The museum was opened in early 1996 as a 90,000 sf facility and an investment of more than $12 million a location prize by comparison to any comparable manufacturing project. It is a noteworthy example also because the location project was a national site search conducted with the assistance of the American Association of Museums (AAM).

The Mighty Eighth's site search team targeted one community where the local economic development office simply showed no interest, apparently because it was not oriented towards assisting with the location of museum projects. I learned about the situation directly from a member of the site selection team, but it was later borne-out by my personal experience in the same community where there was inept handling of a second museum project. As of the writing of this paper, the latter project is still active with four locations under consideration, so I have chosen not to identify it. My point is to stress the importance for communities to orient their economic development towards the full spectrum of opportunities.

In order not to weigh my pursuit of a definition for tourism product totally towards the cultural and heritage interests, I turned to Bill Hardman, Sr., former president of the Southeast Tourism Society, and asked the question, "What is product?" He first defined tourism as the movement of people from one place to another for the purpose of occupying their leisure time in combination with the "...art of entertaining; the promotion of points of interest; and, accommodations for (those) seeking recreation and pleasure." In 1995 Mr. Hardman stated that "tourism product is whatever is put into the promotion." His examples of tourism product ranged from fulfillment pieces to trade shows. He also mentioned that it could be a whole community or an individual facility, such as a park (a site) or a hotel (a property). His definition included events as well as individual efforts to be hospitable and ranged from natural settings to man-made attractions and from public conveyances to pathways.

Mr. Hardman indicated those efforts to put tourism product in place, such as finding a site or property and developing it, are not product development! He said that, instead, "Once the product is in place, the efforts to promote it and put it to use in accordance with tourism definition is product development." He emphatically stated that economic development is the process used to put product in place. After giving consideration to what various people, including those named above, have said and written about tourism product and its development, I concluded that it is what interests travelers and people seeking leisure-time activities.

Product development is the progression from idea to the realization of any one of the categories listed above. My definition incorporates the activities that take place before a product is actually in place; therefore, for practical purposes it includes all of the elements that make it the same as economic development. Expanding on what Mr. Trussell said, tourism product development is setting up and getting ready to ring a cash register with new dollars brought into a community by visitors.

I see product development as a component of economic development. I also see commercial development, community development and industrial development as its components for the purpose of stressing the importance of the whole community as a place for economic development. I believe my argument is strengthened by examination of a definition of economic development from outside of my experience in the business.

Communities that Want to Develop Infrastructure to Attract Tourists

The eight points below is a quick reference for community leaders and economic development practitioners to use to in building programs and setting strategies in place. Links to definitions in the .network glossary for enterprise and economic development are provided. If the interest is in seeking the full spectrum of economic development opportunities, then the first step towards doing things right has already been taken. The best advice that the writer of this resource paper can give is to analyze your community's potential from within as opposed to looking at what has done elsewhere and simply copying a program or strategy. You need to take a best practices approach. For that, it is suggested that you review the the .network summary file: Best Practices for Places that want Economic Development. Keep what you find in that resource as you review the following:

- ❖ The whole community must be developed as a tourist attraction.
- ❖ Understanding the market and its potential is critical to tourism development.
- ❖ The most likely prospects for enterprise development are at the local level.
- ❖ Entrepreneurs become true prospects when investors and developers are added.
- ❖ First-time entrepreneurs and those opening new markets are high-risk prospects.
- ❖ Networking with business suppliers and allies outside the community is smart.
- ❖ Not-for-profit enterprises or attractions can be prospects just like any other.

Public/private partnerships put communities into prospect development.

Enterprise Developers who Need Community Resources and Cooperation

The key words and phrases written into this paper are meant to serve the entrepreneur or business leader who has decisions to make about a community or market he has under consideration. I believe that we are in a time of change when economic development organizations are seriously gearing up to provide complete services to all prospects that offer opportunities to their communities. Prospects need to accept a role in shaping the community economic development organization. I offer the following key words and phrases that I hope will be helpful :

- The real estate industry owns the lead position in commercial development.
- Savvy economic developers work with local real estate professionals.
- When seeking community information, ask for an economic development profile.
- When seeking community data, ask for a checklist for starting-up a new business.
- Tell community leaders what economic impact you expect your project to make.
- Tell economic developers what you want them to guard as confidential information
- Work through trade association(s) to find economic development contacts.
- Network with economic developers who participate in your trade association(s).

CHAPTER-14

RURAL COMMUNITIES AND TOURISM DEVELOPMENT

Community based tourism enables tourists to discover local habitats and wildlife, and celebrates and respects traditional cultures, rituals and wisdom. The community will be aware of the commercial and social value placed on their natural and cultural heritage through tourism, and this will foster community based conservation of these resources. Thanks to responsible tourism and CBT, nature lovers can visit wild areas accompanied by a local guide who explains the traditional uses of the plants and local forest lore, transmitting experience rather than mere information.

Community-based tourism affords travelers with rare opportunities to experience local communities first hand. It's distinctive in that it provides an alternative to development that's not sustainable, giving rural and poor communities an additional source of income. In supporting community-based tourism, you can immerse yourself in the day-to-day lives of local and indigenous people while helping them to preserve their environment and cultural heritage.

The residents earn income as land managers, entrepreneurs, service and produce providers, and employees. At least part of the tourist income is set aside for projects which provide benefits to the community as a whole. Tourists will spend time near areas that are rich in culture and biodiversity, and, at the same time, will get to know the locals at the grassroots level. Many successful experiences in development countries prove that tourism can become a leading sector for the people who conserve natural resources and live on it. Local people of these countries jointly cooperate in Community Based Tourism and this gives not only economic benefits for them but also becomes an example of community involved decision making.

A community by definition implies individuals with some kind of collective responsibility, and the ability to make decisions by representative bodies. Locals' participation, traditional culture, cross-cultural issues and raise of local income are basic principles of tourism and it is fundamental to get more in depth for development countries where tourism is dominantly operate by great foreign companies. Usually families' interviews make obvious that locals are interested to take part in tourism activities but they don't know how.

Often the creation of Community Based Tourism is the best solution for local people or at least a great help for them for example in these countries where the main income is from livestock and the desertification, the spread of unproductive land deprived of vegetation, is one of the main concerns. Community Based Tourism is the jointly planned and managed tourism activities of local group: this new business never can be the main or only income source of the communities and cooperatives but can be additional income possibility. Issues like generating additional incomes for locals and reducing impacts on environment are included in the government policy about tourism, but there has been little implementation and no integrated policy at the national level.

Rural tourism focuses on participating in a rural lifestyle. It can be a variant of ecotourism. Any village can be a tourist attraction, and many villagers are very hospitable. Agriculture is becoming highly mechanized and therefore requires less manual labor. This is causing economic pressure on some villages, leading to an exodus of young people to urban areas.

Rural tourism allows the creation of an alternative source of income in the non-agricultural sector for rural dwellers. The added income from rural tourism can contribute to the revival of lost folk art and handicrafts. It is an ideal and natural method of rural and urban economic exchange. Rural tourism is particularly relevant in developing nations wherein farmland has become fragmented due to population growth. Rural tourism exists in developed nations in the form of providing accommodation in a scenic location ideal for rest and relaxation.

Many niche tourism programs are located in rural areas. From wine tours and eco-tourism, to agritourism and seasonal events, tourism can be a viable economic component in rural community development. According the USDA, Cooperative State, Education and Extension Service, "Tourism is becoming increasingly important to the U.S. economy. A conservative estimate from the Federal Reserve Board in Kansas, based on 2000 data, shows that basic travel and tourism industries accounted for 3.6 percent of all U.S. employment. Even more telling, data from the Travel Industry Association of America indicate that 1 out of every 18 people in the U.S. has a job directly resulting from travel expenditures."

The publication Promoting Tourism in Rural America explains the need for planning and marketing rural community and to weigh the pros and cons of the impacts of tourism. Local citizen participation is helpful and should be included in starting any kind of a tourism program. Being prepared by planning tourism can assist in a successful program that enhances the community.

How is a rural community different from a urban community?

Rural communities are places outside of the cities. For example, if you live in Chicago,IL you live in an urban area. If you live Mendota, IL then you live in a rural area. Thus, urban-city-high population. Rural-towns-low population. Depending on which area you live in, communities are likely to change. In urban areas, there is seen to be a lack of community despite the fact people are living in higher density. A contributing factor to this is, for example, higher crime rates. Still, that does not necessarily mean there is a stronger sense of community in rural areas. In many rural areas, communities are seen as weak because people are cut off from modern technologies, eg. in some countries rural areas cannot access broadband internet or they may have less public transport and so these impact on their social lives. Many rural folk believe that their lives are better though, away from all the smoke and dangers of the city as they think it is a better place to bring up their children, but it may cause just as damaging effects as if they were brought up in urban communities.

Types of Rural Communities

Sociologists have identified a number of different types of rural communities, which have arisen as a result of changing economic trends within rural regions of industrial nations.

The basic trend seems to be one in which communities are required to become entrepreneurial. Those that lack the sort of characteristics mentioned below, are forced to either seek out their niche or accept eventual economic defeat. These towns focus on marketing and public relations whilst bidding for business and government operations; such as, off-site data processing or, perhaps, a factory.

For instance; International Falls, Minnesota markets itself as a site for sub-zero temperature experiments; Ottawa, Illinois managed to attract three Japanese firms; Freeport, Maine has become a center for mail-order companies such as L. L. Bean; and Mobile, Arizona has become the home of a number of solid-waste landfills.

Academic Communities

Academic communities are those in which the primary employers are boarding schools, colleges, universities, research laboratories, and corporate training facilities. These communities bring people away from other regions and thus bring new capital into the area.

Academic institutions, in rural areas, are very much like a factory in that the economic success of the community depends upon the success of the institution. Unlike factories, academic institutions tend to primarily offer jobs in the medium-skilled to professional range.

Area Trade-Centers

The automobile allows rural residents to travel farther, in less time, for goods and services. This reduces the importance of the rural store, along with decreasing rural population. As business relocate from impoverished communities, one town will become the trade center for its region, sometimes doing so by constructing a shopping mall.

Generally, business in a trade-center town, except for those in competition with the mall, will benefit from the mall's presence as shoppers spill over. These trade centers will knock out businesses in, and thus impoverish, nearby towns as shoppers converge on the town with the greatest variety of stores.

Government Centers

Rural regions are undergoing increasing government consolidation. This results in a small number of towns becoming centers of government activity, while the rest are devoid of government infrastructure. These centers include state and local capitals, and areas with prisons or military bases.

Centralized public administration focuses public-sector employment on a single community, assisting it over its neighbors. Benefits, for the government center, include improved public services, increased efficiency, and economic savings.

Recreation Communities

Recreation communities (tourist towns) define some local feature, usually a historic site or scenic vista, as a "natural resource" and market this to tourists. Travelers will then spend money on food, hotels, and the like, which brings capital into the town.

Retirement Communities

Retirement communities tend to house large numbers of elderly people. These retirees, bring pensions, Social Security, and savings which infuse the area with capital. Rural hospitals are increasingly unable to bring enough patients to support their operational budget, and retirement communities have developed, in some areas, as a means to solve this problem. Elderly residents, who migrate from the cities, tend to have above average wealth, thus creating an income disparity between the migrant retirees and the local elderly.

The Effects of Tourism on Local Communities

Can tourism truly be "eco" and if so what are the actual impacts on rural communities? Are we trying to sell something that exists only as a Western concept and if so what are the responsibilities in doing that? Since the Romans arrived in Egypt in 2000BC the African Continent has always attracted "tourists". From the first explorers through to the Big Game Hunters people have come to Africa in search of undiscovered places and ancient cultures seemingly simpler than their own. Post Independence and with pressure from ecologists, many governments set up tourism and wildlife ministries and as wildlife reserves were gazetted, tourism boomed.

The first National Parks were heavily critiqued as a form of "Fortress Conservation"- a playground for colonialists to hunt big game, where wildlife was confined, and local people largely excluded. Package tours brought fresh criticism and the tourism industry began to realise that they were destroying the very nature of what they were selling, the "untouched wilderness" was becoming harder and harder to find. Local communities had often lost land with little compensation or benefit from the tourists who passed daily to view the wildlife they had often lived alongside for generations. The industry reacted and sustainable tourism initiatives began to surface.

This new wave of tourism has attracted a new type of traveler. A traveler who demands more knowledge and who asks more questions, in particular when traveling to developing countries.

Eco-tourism seems to be the buzzword amongst these travellers and is now often generalised as "good tourism", and "mass tourism" tends to be known as "bad tourism". However eco-tourism in particular is a term that can be misunderstood, possibly because it is used as an umbrella term for various tourism activities. Unfortunately all to often it is used for marketing purposes rather than genuinely sustainable tourism initiatives that have long term benefits for local communities.

The Eco Tourism Society definition of eco-tourism is "responsible travel to natural areas that conserves the environment and improves the well-being of local people". However conserving the environment and improving the well being of local people would seem sometimes an unavoidable clash of interests. By conserving the environment, are we always improving the well being of local people? For example, through the gazetting of National Parks, is it more beneficial for a local community to have small permanent plots of land and rely on donations from park entrance fees or use the land nomadically to graze their cattle and trade with local communities? I am not being idealistic or questioning the need and worth of conservation initiatives, I am merely trying to highlight that the question of dependency and the true benefits of tourism and conservation for local communities should be considered.

We truly believe that tourism can bring sustainable development and a route out of the poverty trap so many Africans live in. However, we are also aware that it is hard for all to benefit, so when we get excited about finding another hidden gem in a remote corner of Malawi we try to look around, establish who was there first and who will be affected by us brining visitors there. The research I undertook in Uganda suggested that tourism can bring many developments within a community and greatly increase its economy and infrastructure but it can also breed dependence and a loss of community. Greater wealth often brings greed and without careful handling this can lead to less reliance on one another and instead leave communities with greater disparities of wealth and basic needs than was there before.

Travelers today demand to see more and more remote destinations, they want to travel to areas other tourists have not been too. This is human nature and a wish to be an explorer but it is important to recognise that this search without its pitfalls. When these undiscovered areas are found and tourism moves in, we will surely keep moving away to find newer more remote areas, the demand suggests we will always strive for more wilderness. Therefore we question, are tour operators adding further pressure to fragile environments or are we providing opportunities for development? If so, are we then providing the correct support for communities when tourism comes knocking at the door?

We believe education is a key component to providing sustainable travel experiences both for the visitor and the tour operators. During one of our driver-training sessions we were discussing environmental sustainability and the importance of protecting our environment for future generations. A few of our drivers struggled to link their future generations with our view of protection of land and in particular conservation of wildlife. They appeared far more convinced when we explained issues such as deforestation and depletion of Malawi's natural resources and how this would effect crop production and land use over the coming decades and within their children's lifetime. We would like to think that conservation efforts, in particular National Parks, will be for the future generations of local people as well as international visitors. However, I can't help worrying that potentially the conservation efforts of today will protect a wilderness designed for the tourist and not for the local African. Is this an economical decision? Where the tourist is able to bring valuable capital to the equation, a local Malawian farmer cannot and therefore unknowingly becomes the lowest common denominator.

So what are the responsibilities of tour operators within Africa? Is promoting "eco-tourism" enough? The "sustainable tourism" model is being criticised and dubbed as a new form of colonialism, which imposes conservation on people living at the economic margin, but does it lead to a new form of dependency or is it truly an opportunity to break the vicious cycle of poverty? International models of community and tourism development, in particular in the Dominican Republic and China, could provide ideas and useful policy suggestions to the travel industry and governments. Within Malawi and in other areas of Africa the history of the land and the people often dictates changes to lifestyle.

Therefore a tourism model, which allows for adjustment from situation to situation, may be the way forward and perhaps that needs small operators to work side by side with communities to ensure mutually beneficial initiatives. This would necessitate the travel company to be based within the destination country to ensure that there was updated local knowledge and close links with community projects.

Ecotourism is trying to link the tourism industry with the development movement through ensuring benefits reach the host communities. It is not yet clear whether the tourism industry has the ability to make a considerable impact on poverty alleviation. To achieve this there perhaps needs to be a synergy between the differing stakeholders and the dictates of environmentalism. There needs to be recognition that all forms of tourism leave footsteps and it is where and how we tread that is perhaps important. We are very aware that the field of sustainable travel is yet to be fully understood and we want to make sure we take it piece by piece.

Although it is a conundrum, we have moved forward knowing it is healthy to question, knowing we are ourselves visitors and realising that education is surely the key to sustainable tourism.

BIBLIOGRAPHY

- "AJ Hackett Bungy". Bungy.co.nz. AJHackettBungy. Bungy.co.nz.

- Barzilai, Gad. 2003. Communities and Law: Politics and Cultures of Legal Identities. Ann Arbor: University of Michigan Press.

- Chavis, D.M., Hogge, J.H., McMillan, D.W., & Wandersman, A. 1986. "Sense of community through Brunswick's lens: A first look." Journal of Community Psychology, 14(1), 24-40.

- Chipuer, H. M., & Pretty, G. M. H. (1999). A review of the Sense of Community Index: Current uses, factor structure, reliability, and further development. Journal of Community Psychology, 27(6), 643-658.

- Cymerman, A; Rock, PB. Medical Problems in High Mountain Environments. A Handbook for Medical Officers. USARIEM-TN94-2. US Army Research Inst. of Environmental Medicine Thermal and Mountain Medicine Division Technical Report.

- Durkheim, Émile. 1950 [1895] The Rules of Sociological Method. Translated by S. A. Solovay and J. H. Mueller. New York: The Free Press.

- Eric Larson, 2003 p135, The Devil in the White City; Murder, Magic, and Madness at the Fair that Changed America. Citing Chicago Tribune, Nov. 9, 1889.

- McMillan, D.W., & Chavis, D.M. 1986. "Sense of community: A definition and theory." American Journal of Community Psychology, 14(1), 6-23.

- Mike Barber needed to fly 1% further than Ruhmer's 435 miles (700 km) in order to break the official FAI record; Barber needed to fly only 3 more miles for a total of 440 miles (710 km). Barber's flight remains the longest hang glider flight ever.

- Mountainous plateau creates ozone "halo" around Tibet

- Muza, SR; Fulco, CS; Cymerman, A (2004). "Altitude Acclimatization Guide.". US Army Research Inst. of Environmental Medicine Thermal and Mountain Medicine Division Technical Report (USARIEM-TN-04-05).

- Nancy, Jean-Luc. La Communauté désœuvrée - philosophical questioning of the concept of community and the possibility of encountering a non-subjective concept of it

- Newman, D. 2005. Sociology: Exploring the Architecture of Everyday Life, Chapter 5. "Building Identity: Socialization" Pine Forge Press. Retrieved: 2006-08-05.

- Peck, M.S. 1987. The Different Drum: Community-Making and Peace. New York: Simon and Schuster. ISBN 0-684-84858-9

- Perkins, D.D., Florin, P., Rich, R.C., Wandersman, A. & Chavis, D.M. (1990). Participation and the social and physical environment of residential blocks: Crime and community context. American Journal of Community Psychology, 18, 83-115.

- Putnam, R. D. 2000. Bowling Alone: The collapse and revival of American community. New York: Simon and Schuster

- Sarason, S.B. 1974. The psychological sense of community: Prospects for a community psychology. San Francisco: Jossey-Bass.

- Smith, M. K. 2001. Community. Encyclopedia of informal education. Last updated: January 28, 2005. Retrieved: